# BUILDING A BUSINESS

## THE REAL ESTATE, DESIGN, AND CONSTRUCTION STEPS TO OPENING YOUR RETAIL OR FOOD-SERVICE CONCEPT ON TIME AND ON BUDGET

BY BLAIR RAMSING

# PREFACE

I find great satisfaction in assisting others. When I started helping retail owners get their businesses open, I was frustrated by the lack of information available about the steps and processes involved. Any information was available only in piecemeal fashion, and only rarely was it specific to retail or food-service businesses. There's even less information on what *not* to do, which is equally important. Hence the reason for this book. It highlights the big-picture themes you need to understand and be aware of when building your business.

The information in these pages is derived from my experiences and industry standards. The book runs through the budgeting, real estate, design, construction, signage, and equipment processes needed to get any retail or restaurant concept open on time and on budget while saving time, money, and headaches along the way.

Whether you're opening a one-off enterprise or franchise, a flower shop or a swim center, the steps and procedures are strikingly similar. Whether you're looking to spend $200,000 or $2,000,000, it's all largely the same.

This book does not discuss marketing or operations, because those items are more concept specific, and outside the confines of this book.

Technically, food-service businesses (restaurants, cafés, and bars) are not considered retail. But for the purposes of this book and to streamline writing, mentions of retail include food-service concepts.

After reading the book, feel free to leave a note on my website with questions or comments. Nobody's perfect. I'm far from it. If you believe I've made an error or omission, I'd love to hear from you:
www.blairramsing.com

My website also provides a breakdown of service offerings for anyone in need of assistance or consultation during the development of their store.

# THIS BOOK IS DEDICATED TO YOU

I'd like to thank anyone who's taking the leap of faith and has begun the journey of starting a business. Contrary to popular belief, the big-name corporations are not the driving force of employment: It's small business. The little guys are the heart of the economy and backbone of employment. Small businesses created 65.9 percent of net new jobs in the United States from 2000 to 2017, according to the US Small Business Administration Office of Advocacy [1]. And a 2016 report from Goldman Sachs says half of innovation and product improvements come from small businesses [2]. By starting a business, you're creating jobs, providing goods and services for your community, and making this country great! What a boring world we'd live in without entrepreneurs like you. I wish you success in your endeavors!

I'd like to thank my parents, Kym and Stuart Ramsing. I wouldn't be where I am today without your constant love and support.

# TABLE OF CONTENTS

## Part 1: Funding and Budgets

## Part 2: Real Estate

## Part 3: Design and Architecture

1. The Role of an Architect
2. When to Bring an Architect on Board
3. Finding an Architect
4. Floor Plan
5. Plans (Construction Documents)
6. Producing Plans Pre-Lease
7. Plan Production Time
8. Food-Service Floor Plans
9. Design-Build
10. Plan Costs
11. Franchise Plans
12. Interior Design
13. Owner Versus GC Responsibility to Furnish and Install
14. Sound Abatement
15. Soundproofing
16. Low-Voltage Data
17. Self-Installing Low Voltage
18. Security System
19. Audio System

## Part 4: Permitting

1. Permit Submittal
2. Picking Up Building Permits
3. Physical Plans

## Part 5: Preconstruction

1. What's a General Contractor?
2. Early GC Engagement
3. Ethics of Bidding

## Part 6: Furniture, Fixtures, and Equipment

## Part 7: Signage

Works Cited

# PART 1: FUNDING AND BUDGETS

**Creating a Business Entity**

You've done your research, defined your concept, and created a business plan. First things first: creating a business entity. There are many ways to structure your business, but these are the most common:

1. Sole Proprietorship
2. Partnership
3. Corporation
4. Limited Liability Corporation (LLC)
5. Cooperative

These structures are defined by the laws of the states in which they are formed. A plethora of information on the internet outlines the pros and cons of each. Do your due diligence to find the business entity that's best for your situation.

Not everyone seeks counsel when setting up their business entity, but it never hurts to consult with a business attorney, especially if you wish to raise capital by distributing shares of your company or multiple partners, stakeholders, or investors will be involved.

**Project Budget**

Architects exclude project-cost estimating from their scope of services. In limited instances an architect may provide rudimentary construction-cost estimates only. Estimating project costs is a difficult undertaking, even for a seasoned project manager or consultant who's estimated multiple concepts of a similar nature.

First-time business owners tend to discount the actual cost of opening a retail store. There's a tendency to underestimate costs of known items, and a host of "unknowns" always surface during development. They say opening a retail business for first-timers costs twice as much and takes three times as long as initially anticipated. This often rings true for business owners who fail to properly research and construct their budget. Do your due diligence and be realistic about costs.

So that you don't fall prey to underfunding your venture, consider the following when producing a budget:

1. **Do actual project-cost research.** Don't just assume your signage will cost $2,000 because "$2,000 seems like a reasonable number." A ton of information is available online. Further, consider calling vendors to get real estimates.

2. **Include the totality of an item's cost.** Nowadays many people's budgets are heavily reliant on comparative internet pricing. For bulky equipment and furniture found online, the landed cost (or total price after receiving the product) can easily be 20–40 percent more after factoring in shipping and sales tax.

Does your furniture, fixtures, and equipment (FF&E) require additional costs such as unpacking and installation? Odds are decent that by the time your FF&E arrive, you'll be focused on marketing, operations, and store hiring, with no time to unpack and install your equipment. It often takes longer than you'd think. Contractors and equipment vendors are happy to do it, but they typically charge $2,000 to $6,000, depending on the scope of work.

3. **Reach out to family or friends who have opened a retail business.** Have them review your numbers. Even if their concept differs from yours, there will be overlapping commonalities between design, construction, and services costs. For instance, your friend's pet shop and your antiques store both require merchant services and a website. They'll be able to identify these costs and others you may not have considered. They'll also be able to advise you about potential discrepancies between your budget and actual prices based on their experience.

4. **Work with a consultant.** This is a common task of consultants. Odds are decent they've already spent many hours researching costs for clients and seen project costs for a multitude of concepts, including something similar to yours. A good consultant will have a general knowledge of all costs, from point-of-sale (POS) systems to restroom sinks.

5.  **Join your local chamber of commerce or small-business association's community group.** Some organizations are better than others, depending on your city, but the right business networks can provide a gold mine of resources and mentors to advise on start-up costs.

6.  **Visit a concept similar to yours.** Look around and take note of the store's décor and FF&E. Take pictures if you can. This will uncover items you hadn't thought of, such as the A-frame sign outside the business, the "open hours" graphics on their door, and those gift cards and business cards at the check-out stand.

There are many ways to draft a budget, depending on how you allocate funds from one budgetary bucket to another, whether you decide to pay a millworker or offset that work onto your general contractor, and how specific you get. I've seen budget worksheets that are thousands of line items long, with every known cost earmarked down to the most minute of details, such as the costs of pencils and paper. I've also seen budgets only thirty lines long. Try to be as detailed as possible. The more time you spend researching what's needed, the more items you'll inevitably uncover that you hadn't previously considered.

Once you've "completed" your budget, set it aside for a week or two, then review it with a fine-tooth comb. Like writing an email, putting it aside for a period of time and then looking at your work with a fresh set of eyes will always uncover items that were initially missed or found to be incorrect.

When drafting your budget, start by determining the main project costs. For most of these main categories, no specific cost should be assigned. Rather, cost should be derived from the subcomponents of the categories. The generic budget example below appears to have approximately 60 lines. In actuality there are over 300, since most of the categories have subcategories with additional items.

For instance, the Marketing category has two subcategories, but within those subcategories are many single-line cost estimates. The Marketing's Grand Opening and Promotions subcategory has $5,000 that may be based on costs such as production and distribution of door hangers, social media advertising, mailers, grand-opening-day giveaways, paid commercials, grand-opening-day entertainment, and more.

Your store's FF&E subcategory often contains the highest number of costs, often 100–300 items! To keep your FF&E (or any other large budget section) organized and user-friendly, consider breaking it into 5–10 sections such as Furniture, Fixtures, Equipment, Paid Services, POS and Technology, Office Supplies, and Smallwares. Some people prefer to categorize their FF&E by store area, such as Patio, Office, Retail Floor, Supply Room, Restrooms, and Purchase Area. Do whatever suits your style.

If you're getting a Small Business Administration (SBA) loan or a conventional loan, be cognizant of loan-closing costs. Some lenders wrap these costs into the overall loan, but many don't. You may be required to pay loan attorney fees, origination fees (or packaging fees), title and closing costs, and guarantee fees. On a $300,000 loan, you could easily pay $15,000 to $25,000 in up-front loan-closing fees.

| BLAIR'S BURGER BAR PROJECTED OPENING COSTS | | Cost | % |
|---|---|---|---|
| 1 | **Real Estate Costs** | **$ 19,650.00** | **3.76%** |
| | Real estate deposit | $ 6,200.00 | |
| | 2 months' rent @ $6,200 per month | $ 12,400.00 | |
| | 2 months' CAM's @ $1,050 per month | $ 1,050.00 | |
| 2 | **Construction** | **$252,000.00** | **48.24%** |
| | General construction | $ 225,000.00 | |
| | Millwork | $ 8,500.00 | |
| | Lighting package | $ 11,000.00 | |
| | Low voltage data | $ 7,500.00 | |
| 3 | **Storefront Signage and Graphics** | **$ 9,200.00** | **1.76%** |
| | Backlit storefront sign - 3' x 9' | $ 4,500.00 | |
| | Backlit blade sign - 2' x 4' | $ 1,900.00 | |
| | Two monument signs @ $750 each | $ 1,500.00 | |
| | Window graphics and store hours | $ 1,300.00 | |
| 4 | **FF&E (Furnitures, Fixtures & Equipment)** | **$150,450.00** | **28.80%** |
| | Furniture | $ 28,500.00 | |
| | Fixtures | $ 16,650.00 | |
| | Equipment | $ 83,250.00 | |
| | Paid services | $ 2,600.00 | |
| | POS and technology | $ 5,200.00 | |
| | Office supplies | $ 2,500.00 | |
| | Smallwares | $ 11,750.00 | |
| 5 | **Professional Services** | **$ 41,450.00** | **7.93%** |
| | Accounting | $ 1,500.00 | |
| | A&E - architecture and engineering | $ 13,750.00 | |
| | Permit submittal by professional (consultant, architect, or permit handler) + $500 printing and | $ 1,750.00 | |
| | Site survey + travel expenses | $ 3,300.00 | |
| | Liquor attorney | $ 3,000.00 | |
| | Commercial lease attorney | $ 2,500.00 | |
| | Construction contract attorney | $ 1,500.00 | |
| | Consultant and project management | $ 11,500.00 | |
| | Website design, domain, web hosting, emails, etc. | $ 2,650.00 | |

15

| | | | |
|---|---|---:|---:|
| 6 | **Opening Inventory** | **$ 27,500.00** | **5.26%** |
| | Opening liquor and beer order | $ 13,000.00 | |
| | Opening food order | $ 9,500.00 | |
| | Merchandise | $ 3,500.00 | |
| | Chemicals and supplies | $ 1,500.00 | |
| 7 | **Marketing** | **$ 8,000.00** | **1.53%** |
| | Grand opening and promotions | $ 5,000.00 | |
| | 3 months' pre-open marketing @ $1000 per month | $ 3,000.00 | |
| 8 | **Insurance** | **$ 1,800.00** | **0.34%** |
| | 3 Months' pre-open @ $600 per month | $ 1,800.00 | |
| 9 | **Personnel Expenses** | **$ 5,400.00** | **1.03%** |
| | Pre-open management training - 10 days | $ 1,600.00 | |
| | Pre-open staff training payroll - 7 days | $ 3,800.00 | |
| 10 | **Business Licenses and Permits** | **$ 7,550.00** | **1.45%** |
| | Building permit | $ 3,500.00 | |
| | Signage permit | $ 850.00 | |
| | Liquor license - 2 year license @ $1,100 per year | $ 2,200.00 | |
| | Misc. business licenses and permits | $ 1,000.00 | |
| 11 | **Utilities and Deposits** | **$ 1,200.00** | **0.23%** |
| 12 | **Lending Costs** | **$ 18,200.00** | **3.48%** |
| | Title and closing cost | $ 5,500.00 | |
| | Lending attorney fee | $ 2,200.00 | |
| | SBA guaranty fee (3% of loan amount) | $ 9,000.00 | |
| | Packaging fee | $ 1,500.00 | |
| 13 | **Additional Funds ~ 15%** | **$ 80,000.00** | **15.31%** |
| 14 | **Estimated Project Cost Before Receiving Tenant Improvement Allowance** | **$622,400.00** | |
| 15 | **Tenant Improvement Allowance** | **$100,000.00** | **19.14%** |
| 16 | **Estimated Project Cost After Receiving Tenant Improvement Allowance of $100,000** | **$522,400.00** | **100.00%** |

No matter how you come up with your project budget, understand that it's an *estimate*, and actual costs *will* differ. *Always* have additional funds that can be tapped in the event of budgetary overruns.

People often blow their budgets because they allocate buckets of monies to cost categories without following through on what those categories have in them or fail to research item costs. I can't blame them. It's a tedious task to get costs for all your store's items, but it's the best way to account for cost. By spending the time to research costs for all opening budget items, you may just find that you need more items than you initially anticipated, and that some of those pieces are more expensive than you initially envisioned.

No matter how thorough you are with your opening budget, there will *always* be items that you won't know you need until after you've created it. Projects also tend to be prolonged, resulting in additional professional service costs or "dark rent" payments (rent on a space that's not yet open). Additionally, we have a natural tendency to discount costs [3] [4]. Because of these realities, consider adding 15 to 20 percent of "additional funds" above and beyond the anticipated project cost to your budget. Better to have it and not need it!

In the budget example you'll notice I've allocated funds for three months of pre-open rent. Why? Although landlords often provide an initial free-rent period, it's typically not enough to get your doors open on time. Odds are good you'll pay some "dark rent." Even if you're one of the fortunate few who open without paying dark rent, the first months (even years) of operating a new business can net slim profits as you're growing the business. Having monies allocated for start-up rent will help alleviate early cash-flow strains.

### Receiving Tenant Improvement Allowance

Landlords often provide a tenant improvement (TI) allowance to go toward leasehold improvements (construction). These funds will be distributed in accordance to your lease stipulations. In most instances, you'll receive 50–100 percent of the funds only after construction is complete and you've provided the landlord with the necessary construction close-out documents, which can take four to eight weeks.

Once the landlord has their close-out documents, they typically have 15 to 30 days to release your tenant improvement allowance. Although a landlord may provide a portion of your TI allowance upon the commencement of construction, that's atypical, and I've never seen this amount exceed 33 to 50 percent of the total funds provided. This means you'll be required to float most, if not all, of your project costs while you're waiting for the landlord to release your TI allowance. This is *critical* to understand. Too often a business owner will see their project cost as being, say, $500,000. Since they're getting $100,000 from their landlord, they figure they'll need only $400,000. In reality, they need $450,000 to $500,000, since their landlord is releasing most or possibly all of their TI allowance many weeks or months after they've opened for business.

### Construction Budget

The construction portion of a budget is a big piece of the pie—often 35 to 65 percent of the overall project budget.

Underestimating construction costs can blow the whole budget. Accurately estimating construction cost is difficult, because when you're drafting a budget, you've not yet engaged with an architect to produce plans or taken those plans to contractors for hard bids. You've likely only conceptualized what your store will look like, and you know its general size. Since that's all you have to work with, you have three options:

1. Find a contractor or proprietor who has built a concept similar to yours and ask them what it cost to build. I prefer to seek costs from the proprietor.

2. Get an *estimate* from a contractor based on the type of concept, square footage, proposed work, and finishes you hope to see, and the condition of the space you anticipate receiving from a landlord. For example, will the landlord have already installed HVAC units and electrical panels? (See "Space Condition" below for further information.)

3. Work with a consultant. Unlike a contractor who may be telling you what you want to hear, a consultant will generally give you a more accurate account of the cost.

Regardless of how you come up with your estimated construction cost, it's important to understand and factor in the next four sections: "Construction Costs Over Time," "GC Cost Estimates," "Estimate Versus Quote," and "Space Condition."

**Construction Costs Over Time**

As of the writing of this book—Q1, 2019—the construction industry has been white-hot, with the cost of materials and labor outpacing inflation nearly every year since the Great Recession of 2009, per the National Bureau of Economic Research. From July 2010 to July 2018, nonresidential construction costs rose 21.47 percent [5] while the broader US inflation rate rose 15.2 percent [6].

The increase in building costs has not been distributed equally. Although some areas, primarily the Midwest and South (excluding Texas) have experienced moderate cost increases, much of the East and West Coast have seen construction costs surpass the national average, jumping 30 percent or more during the same period of 2010 to 2018. Nonresidential construction costs in Seattle rose 40.2 percent [7] during this time period. Cities such as Portland, Oregon; Denver; San Francisco; and Dallas have seen similar cost increases [8]. That means your friend's yoga studio in Seattle that cost $250,000 to construct in 2010 would cost $350,500 to build in 2018!

Increases in construction costs have only accelerated in recent years. A retail concept built in Denver with construction costing $400,000 in 2014 would cost $490,920 to build in 2018, just four years later [9]!

When estimating your business's construction costs, be mindful of the economic conditions in the area where you're building. If you're basing your store's construction in part on a similar concept that was built a few years ago, make sure you factor in rising costs, because you won't be able to build anything for the price of yesteryear.

Some cost indexes for large cities are available for free online. If you're building in a small city, you may have to pay to access the data. RS Means has arguably the most extensive construction-cost databases. Although they have an abundance of city cost data, much of their data centers on specific building material and installation pricing, which is quite helpful when deciding what finishes or fixtures to use. Heads-up: Many of their books cost $250 to $500, with data at times being technical in nature to decipher.

### General Contractor (GC) Cost Estimates

When getting estimates from contractors, understand that their numbers will be off the mark from actual cost. In my experience, GCs typically underestimate projects, and sometimes by wide margins. Why is this? There are a few reasons:

1. Humans are inherently optimistic, with a tendency to underestimate costs [3] [4].
2. Some GCs will tell you what you want to hear, not what you need to hear. This means if a general contractor gives you an estimate for your construction that's lower than that of other GCs, guess who you'll continue to work with?
3. Some general contractors are just poor estimators. They can be great at building things, and they know their own cost, but they're not always tuned in to their subcontractors' costs (which makes up the majority of a GC's bid).

### Estimate Versus Quote

It's important to understand the difference between an estimate and a quote. Merriam-Webster defines an estimate as "the act of appraising or valuing" [10]. In other terms, an estimate is an approximation or best guess. Estimates are typically nonbinding, with the price subject to change based on additional details and information.

A quote (sometimes referred to as a bid or proposal) is an offer to provide a service at a specific price point.

Even though these terms and their definitions are generally agreed upon throughout business, there can be confusion. Not sure whether a price is firm or approximate? Get clarification.

For construction pricing, any numbers that are based on a physical set of architecture and engineering (A&E) plans are typically quotes, whereas costs that are not based on actual plans are estimates that are subject to change.

**Space Condition**

A big part of construction estimating that's often overlooked is factoring in the condition of the space you're receiving from the landlord. I don't put any stock in real estate brokers or landlords who say a space is in "cold gray shell" or "vanilla shell" condition. (Other terms include *gray shell*, *cold shell*, *warm vanilla shell*, and *white box*.) These terms are used interchangeably, and quite frankly, no real estate people and few landlords truly understand the difference between them. In theory, a "cold gray shell" is a space being turned over to a tenant with little more than exterior walls, a ceiling, and basic utilities run to the retail space, whereas a "warm vanilla shell" has all sorts of building attributes already built. Unfortunately, there's no agreed-upon standard definition from one term to another. Brokers and landlords will market any space as being in "vanilla" or "warm vanilla" condition, because it sounds more appealing.

Terminology aside, it's difficult to determine construction costs because you could be looking at two seemingly identical spaces across the street from each other that are the same square footage, yet one might cost $150,000 to construct and the other $300,000. You heard it right: You receive the same final product, using the same finishes and fixtures, but one is twice the cost to build. How is this possible? In reality, every location has a different amount of work needed.

Dozens of factors affect the cost of building a retail concept. Have items like the sprinkler system, storefront glass, insulation, demising walls (the shared walls between neighboring tenants), interior slab, and electrical, mechanical, telephone and data, water, sewage, gas, and fire alarm systems already been constructed by the landlord? If so, you've likely got a true "warm vanilla shell." Are existing site attributes sufficient for your use, or do they require modifications or upgrades? If upgrades are needed or new utilities need to be run to the space, how far away is the distribution point? Are there any water or sewage tap fees (costs to access the city's infrastructure)? Are you in a single-story or multistory building?

As you can see, many factors and site attributes dramatically affect the cost of building a concept. The considerations are numerous in scope and technical in nature, so consider working with a consultant (or possibly an architect) when determining your construction budget!

**Project Funding**

Once you've determined a budget, you'll need to decide how you'll fund the project. Common funding avenues are listed below. To increase your odds of receiving a loan from any lender, having good credit (a score above 650), putting personal funds toward the project (at least 25 percent), having a background in the type of business you hope to open, or entering an established franchise organization will increases your odds of securing a loan.

1. **Self-funding**—This is the path of least resistance. If you can fund the project with your own capital, you'll be saving yourself money (by avoiding loan interest and closing costs) and lots of time on paperwork and middleman facilitators.

2. **SBA loan**—A Small Business Administration (SBA) loan is the second most common financing avenue for those seeking a loan. SBA loans are provided by banks, with a portion of the loan backed by the federal government. With less stringent borrowing requirements compared with their conventional loan counterparts, SBA loans typically have higher interest rates. The 7(a) loan is what you'll need, assuming you're borrowing more than $50,000. SBA loans require personal guarantees (which are discussed later in this chapter).

3. **Conventional loan**—Conventional lenders are the most common financing avenue, with loans typically provided by banking institutions (like an SBA loan). Unlike SBA loans, they're not

backed by the government. The approval process is generally quicker and less laborious than with an SBA loan, since conventional lenders have more stringent eligibility stipulations, such as higher credit score requirements. Conventional lending structures are often more lenient in the loan structure and interest rates are generally lower than SBA loans (although many SBA lenders will claim to have the lowest interest rates).

Both traditional lenders and SBA lenders require new businesses to have "approximately one dollar of cash or business assets for each three dollars of the loan" [11]. Therefore, if you're looking to spend $400,000 in total project funds, you'll need to put $100,000 of your own capital toward the project, with the lender funding the remaining $300,000.

4. **Personal loan**—Personal loans from family, friends, or acquaintances have their upsides: quicker to acquire, less paperwork, and often more favorable loan terms (assuming there are any) compared with banking lenders. The downside? If you're unable to repay a personal loan, it can destroy your relationship with the lender. Ruined relationships aside, don't borrow from someone who's putting everything on the line. If you're unable to pay them back, they'll go bust. A lending institution won't. Having a bankrupt friend or family member is not something you want on your

conscience. Heaven forbid that happens; you'll wish you had borrowed from an institution.

5.  **Grants**—A grant won't fully fund your venture, but consider seeing if there are any available. Private philanthropists, corporations, and city governments grant money to spur economic development in depressed areas and create jobs. Do an internet search for "small-business grants." There are some grants specifically for women, veterans, minorities, and other groups who are underrepresented in business.

    Getting a grant is no walk in the park. You may spend hours applying for multiple grants, with nothing coming to fruition. If you do receive a grant, it may come with certain spending requirements and detailed accountings of how funds are to be spent. But hey, free money is free money. Never look a gift horse in the mouth.

    The federal government is one of the largest grant givers. Visit Grants.gov and search "small business." Federal grants are generally focused on spurring technological innovation, health care advancements, and education. As such, there may be multiple applicable grants for a solar installation company or learning center concept, but little to nothing available for an art studio or flower boutique.

If you've decided to acquire an SBA or conventional loan, shop around, because rates and service levels vary. I've worked with clients whose lenders made the loan process easy (all things considered). I've also had clients whose lenders made the process a nightmare—always working with a different loan officer or needing to sort through miles of restrictions whenever draw payments to the client's vendors were needed.

Assuming you're seeking an SBA or conventional loan, get a pre-approval letter from the bank *before* locking into a lease. A pre-approval letter says that based on your current financial condition and the broader economic state of affairs, the bank would lend you a certain amount of money.

A bank may pre-approve you for a loan, then reject you or decrease the loan amount at the time you actually apply for it if your personal financial condition worsens, your money goes from liquid to fixed, or negative macroeconomic events occur, such as a liquidity freeze in financial markets. A pre-approval letter isn't "money in the bank," but assuming your finances stay rosy, odds are good you'll get the loan when you need it.

A landlord may not request a pre-approval letter, but the pre-approval amount is an important indicator of whether your needed borrowing level will support your project budget and whether you can really afford the real estate you're contemplating.

**Personal Finances and Personal Guarantee**

The better your personal finances, the better your chances of securing good real estate. Landlords want to see high net worth, and primarily, liquidity. Why? Because even if your business goes south, having money in the bank means you'll still make rent payments.

If it comes down to choosing between your "cool" concept and a lackluster Joe Shmoe's Cleaners, many landlords will take the lackluster concept because Joe Shmoe has better finances than you. Many landlords would prefer to lease to a deep-pocketed Joe Shmoe at $36 per square foot rather than accept your offer of $38 per square foot at full asking price.

What's more, a tenant with "weak" finances may be required to pay a security deposit upon execution of the lease equal to two or even three times the monthly rental rate versus a tenant with strong finances who may be required to pay a deposit equal to only one month's rent. In commercial real estate, money talks and bullshit walks.

"Why does the landlord want to see my personal finances?" you ask. "I'll be running everything through a corporation or LLC. If the business goes bad, it's only my business entity that goes bust. My personal finances and assets will be sheltered."

Unfortunately, you're not the first to think of that, which is why personal guarantees exist—and you'll likely be required to agree to one when signing a lease. If you're leasing during good economic times, a personal guarantee is almost impossible to get out of. Why? In good times, there's greater real estate demand. Since it takes years for real estate supply to match demand, landlords can call the shots, thus requiring tenants to sign personal guarantees. What does this mean? If your business entity goes bust, the landlord can come after your personal assets—cars, houses, bank accounts, you name it.

Some landlords will agree to a personal guarantee "burn-off," meaning that after a certain amount of time (often three to five years), the personal guarantee will become null and void if the tenant makes all rent payments on time during the agreed-upon term.

Be cautious about trying to get out of a personal guarantee. Not only are they industry standard, but agreeing to a personal guarantee shows that you steadfastly believe in your concept. Trying to maneuver out of a personal guarantee may send a signal to your landlord that you don't believe in your concept or yourself.

# PART 2: REAL ESTATE

**Space Attributes**

The first part of the real estate process involves defining the space attributes and site criteria needed for your business. These include items such as the following:

1. **Square footage**—What size space should you seek? If you're not sure, see "Floor Plan" in part 3. You may need to have an architect draft a generic space plan to find the minimum and maximum square footage that your business requires. Alternatively, you can seek out similar concepts and ask those concepts' proprietors what their square footage is. When talking to the owner, pick their brains on what their ideal square footage would be if they were to do it over again. Alternatively, you can work with a consultant who may have previous experience with concepts similar to yours.

2. **Location**—Urban, rural, downtown, or suburban. What are your search-area parameters?

3. **Building type**—Shopping center, mall, or standalone (single-tenant building)

4. **Minimum ceiling height**—Some concepts such as fine dining or children's play centers require ceilings higher than the standard 12–15-foot height that you'll find in many commercial retail spaces.

5. **Patio**—Does your concept require a patio? Certain markets with year-round temperate weather afford continual patio use. Because of this, landlords in temperate climates may require tenants to pay rent on the patio area in addition to the interior space. In most markets, though, you don't pay any additional cost for patio area, so even if your concept doesn't require a patio, consider seeking a space with one: It only adds value!

6. **Drive-thru window**—Does your concept require a drive-thru window?

7. **End cap versus in-line**—In a shopping center, in-line spaces have tenants on either side of them. Just like it sounds, end-cap spaces are at the ends of a retail center and have tenants on only one side of them. The benefits to end caps include additional window space, additional signage space, and, depending on where it's situated, often better visibility to passersby. Since many concepts rely on accessibility and ease of use, the additional side of parking that end caps often can be important. End-cap rents are often higher than those of their in-line counterparts.

8. **Approved zoning use**—Different properties and buildings have different approved uses. It's costly and timely to attempt to change a building's zoning use. Find out what kind of use your concept requires. If you come across a commercial space with zoning that differs from your concept requirements, go to your local planning department after receiving landlord approval and speak with a zoning expert to determine whether it's possible to rezone the space, and what it will take. If you're attempting to rezone a property to a more "lucrative" zoning classification, your landlord might help with the cost of rezoning their property.

Still not sure what site attributes are best for your concept or if your business has special needs? Seek advice from a consultant, architect, or broker. Talking to owners of similar concepts can also provide a trove of good insight. Ask them what they like about their location, and what they would have done differently.

**Using a Broker**

A commercial real estate broker provides listings for their clients to view. Brokers also facilitate the process of securing real estate through letter-of-intent (LOI) negotiations and lease negotiations. Broker services typically come at no cost to the client, because landlords often pay a 2–3 percent commission to both the client's broker and the listing agent.

In the internet age, some people forgo the use of a broker, since you can find commercial real estate online. Although you could go it alone, using a seasoned broker will get you in front of spaces that are not yet online—the coveted spaces. A good broker will bring industry perspective, local market knowledge, network connections, and negotiating experience. Because this option doesn't cost you anything, it's the recommended avenue.

One of the best ways to find a great broker is to call your local commercial brokerage firm and ask to speak with the broker who is most requested (or signs the most annual deals). This person is popular for a reason: They get deals done, they're experienced, and clients like them! On top of that, they're sure to be well connected with a large network of developers and landlords. Alternatively, you can seek recommendations from local business owners, preferably owners of concepts similar to yours. If you're still drawing a blank, do an internet search. CBRE is the world's largest commercial real estate services firm with a presence in most US markets. They also have a large trove of demographic analytics.

Some brokers are better than others. Consider qualifying (or vetting) a broker before using them. Ask the broker for recent client references, and call those references to see how their experience went. Finding commercial real estate for retail can take many months, even years. Make sure you've got a good broker on board for the ride. A good broker should be able to get you in front of the right spaces and speed up the process. A great broker will continue to send you new prospective spaces even after you've found a space you like!

## Touring Your Market

When you bring a broker on board, let them know that within two to three days you'd like to have at least 15 potential spaces on paper to review. Within a week of bringing a broker on board, you should do a real estate tour with them, walking through each location you're interested in. Share a car with the broker and spend time between tours picking their brain about what they think of each space. Your broker may see different pros and cons that you didn't consider.

When finding real estate, challenge yourself to tour at least five spaces, preferably more. Too often, people have a preconceived location in mind or get fixated on the first location they visit. When you force yourself to look at multiple spaces, things come to light that you hadn't contemplated. Sometimes that first "gotta-have" space becomes less attractive as you start to size it up against other locations that have more parking, greater visibility, or easier left-turn-in access.

## Site Attributes

Rate prospective spaces you've toured based on site attributes. Below are some common site attributes to consider:

1. **Demographics**—Most brokers can provide one-, three-, and five-mile demographic studies with detailed information on age, income, race, population, and the number of households or businesses. The immediate area's demographics (demos) should match your concept's target audience. Place greater

importance on the one-mile demos and less on the five-mile demos. Consumers do most of their shopping and spending in the immediate area around which they live and work. Not surprisingly, consumers also repatronize nearby establishments at a higher frequency. A study by Access Development found that 93.2 percent of consumers travel 20 minutes or less to make their everyday purchases, and 87 percent travel 15 minutes or less [12]. Based on the survey results, you could surmise that 50 percent or more of consumers travel less than five to seven minutes from their home or place of work to make their purchases.

2. **Traffic count**—The more traffic passing by your space, the more potential for business. Count the foot and vehicle traffic passing by potential spaces over a 60-minute window during both busy and slow traffic times that are applicable to your store's open hours. Traffic counts are not perfect. They can't tell demographics, and you'll get different traffic counts on holidays, weekdays versus weekends, and during different weather. Nonetheless, traffic counts are a good measure of comparative traffic levels from one location to the next. Do traffic counts for prospective locations during similar days and times.

3. **Accessibility**—Is there easy left-turn-in access? When leaving, how about left-turn-out? Having signals at intersections leading to shopping-center entrances is a plus. Convenience is key.

You'll lose customers when leasing spaces with difficult ingress and egress.

4. **Parking**—This is often overlooked, but it's another big consideration. Is there adequate parking during busy periods? Is parking free and unrestricted? Are parking spaces adequately sized? How many shopping centers do you avoid because of a lack of parking, pay-to-park only, or tight spots that are tough to fit a truck or SUV into? It comes down to ease and *convenience* for customers. See the theme? Although it's not ideal to lease from a shopping center with lots of parking spaces restricted for other tenants, it doesn't hurt to ask the landlord for dedicated parking for your customers. Landlords are typically amenable to providing dedicated parking spaces for businesses with lots of carryout business.

5. **Visibility**—Nothing beats visibility. It's free marketing that works for you 24/7. Will your storefront signage be clearly visible to passing foot and vehicle traffic? The difference in visibility between an end cap next to a roadway and in-line space just one door down can be huge.

6. **Co-tenant pros and cons**—Are co-tenants noisy? Are they "dull" or "exciting"? Would you consider co-tenants competitors or complimentary to your business? Co-tenants are important because their customers walk past your doors! Figure out when your business's peak hours are, and then find co-

tenants with peak hours that differ from yours. This increases business for your store during slow hours. If you're in an industry that's busy in the late afternoon or evening, you want co-tenants such as coffee shops, nail salons, or insurance companies that have mostly morning and midday business.

7. **Center occupancy**—Is the shopping center filled, partially filled, or empty? The fuller the better. Is there high traffic count entering your center? Bustling shopping centers increase the odds of spillover business for all tenants.

8. **Surrounding development**—The denser the surrounding area, the better for business. Being the first into a new development usually isn't good. Nearby lots that are soon to be developed will boost your stores sales, but not today. It takes time to build, then fill up new development. None of that helps you pay your first month's or year's rent. What's worse, heavy development means heavy construction, which causes headaches for nearby businesses and creates areas to avoid for drivers and those on foot. Remember what Daymond John says: "Pioneers get slaughtered; settlers prosper."

9. **Previous tenants**—What's the track record of previous tenants? Chronic turnover is a sign of something awry: poor visibility, high rent, or just a bad area. Oddly enough, high turnover can create a stigma around a "cursed" space or area that consumers will want to avoid.

**Know When to Spend the Money**

Even in this digital age, visibility is key. Although more expensive, a space with good visibility and easy access should be sought for customer-oriented businesses, which includes virtually all retail and food-service concepts. Paying increased rent for greater visibility allows you to put more of your time and money toward growing the business rather than marketing your business to let the world know of your existence. With that said, know what fair market costs for your area are, and more importantly, determine the maximum rental rate your business model supports.

**LOI Template**

When you find real estate you're seriously interested in, you'll need to submit a letter of intent (LOI) to the landlord's agent. Submitting an LOI on a space means submitting an offer to lease the space. The LOI indicates your proposed rental rate and rental terms, and outlines the expected framework of the lease. Unlike a lease that can be 50 to 100 pages long, the LOI is much shorter, typically just 1 to 6 pages. Listed below are generic items to include in an LOI for retail concepts. Work with your broker or a consultant to determine specific criteria required for your business.

1. **Tenant**—Provide tenant's legal entity name, DBA name, home address, phone number, and email address.
2. **Landlord**—Provide landlord and landlord representative's name and contact information.
3. **Broker**—Provide tenant representative's name and contact information.

4. **Guarantor**—Include verbiage on whether tenant will personally guarantee the lease and for how long. For example, *Tenant's principals shall personally guarantee the base rent and additional charges for the first three (3) years of the base term.*

5. **Premises**—Provide address and unit or suite number of the desired retail space.

6. **Square footage**—Provide desired square footage (including square footage of patio if applicable).

7. **Use**—Describe tenant's use of the space. For example, *Fiona's Flowers will occupy the space to conduct the business of assembling flower bouquets and gift merchandise for retail sale.*

8. **Primary rent term**—Provide initial term of lease. An initial term between 5 and 10 years is standard. Landlords will provide a greater tenant improvement allowance for tenants who accept a 10-year lease, because it gives landlords more time to recoup the TI dollars they're providing. A tenant's willingness to enter a 10-year lease also gives landlords confidence in the tenant's commitment.

9. **Base rental rate**—Include proposed base rental rate.

10. **Annual rent adjustment**—Include proposed annual rent increase to account for Inflation. For example, *The base rental rate shall increase at a rate of two percent (2 percent) per annum.*

11. **Options**—Include renewal options. Two, three, or four five-year extension periods is common. For example, *The initial term of lease shall be ten (10)*

*years. Tenant shall have the option to renew for three (3) additional five (5) year terms.*

12. **Additional rent**—In addition to the base rental rate, you'll be required to pay your proportion of the retail center's operating expenses such as taxes, insurance, and common-area maintenance (CAM) fees. A landlord will provide an estimated additional rent amount, which tenants must pay on a monthly basis. After end-of-year reconciliations, the landlord will credit or charge the tenant accordingly for any additional monies. For example, *First-year additional rent is not to exceed $3.75 per square foot. Controllable additional rent increases are to be capped at no more than 2.5 percent per annum.*

13. **Possession**—Input the date the landlord is to provide possession of the space to tenant.

14. **Rent commencement**—Input date of rent commencement (when rent payments begin). Most landlords provide a "free-rent" or "rent abatement" period while tenants are designing and constructing their space. Free-rent periods vary based on local market conditions. A typical free-rent period is 90–150 days from either the execution of the lease or the date the tenant receives building permits. Since it can take 30–60 days to create plans, then another 45–180 days to receive building permits, *it's best to try to peg the rent commencement date off the receival of building permits date,* even if it means accepting a lesser free-rent period. For example, *Rent shall*

*commence 90 days after tenant receives building permits.*

15. **Landlord requirements**—Include landlord site maintenance and upkeep responsibility. For example, *Landlord shall keep all exterior and structural conditions in good working order and presentation.*

16. **Signage**—Landlords typically have the prerogative on signage requirements, because they have certain standards for all tenants to adhere to. Regardless, request storefront signage on each side of the building's façade, scaled to the maximum allowable size permitted per local code. Request optimal space for the monument sign and use of a "Coming Soon" banner.

17. **Parking**—Provide parking criteria. For example, *All parking shall be unrestricted and free of charge.*

18. **Contingency**—This provides a back-out clause for the tenant after the execution of the lease if the tenant is unable to acquire the necessary permits. For example, *If tenant has not received such governmental permits and approvals within 120 days (after showing reasonable attempts were made), tenant, at its option, may terminate the lease, at which point landlord shall return all prepaid deposits in full.*

19. **Exclusive**—Provide any desired exclusive-use terms (see "Noncompete Clauses" below).

20. **Tenant improvement allowance**—Landlords typically provide a tenant improvement allowance (commonly "TI" or "TIA") to go toward leasehold improvements (construction costs). TI allowances

very significantly based on local market conditions and the turnover condition of the space. Landlords typically offer more TI allowance for spaces without storefronts, demising walls (the shared wall between two tenants), HVAC, proper plumbing and electrical, a concrete floor, and interior insulation. Tenant improvement allowances can vary from $0 per square foot to $80 per square foot or more.

21. **Landlord work letter**—The "landlord work letter" is a subsection of a retail lease outlining the proposed condition of the space a tenant will receive. Landlords routinely run utilities or install basic systems for tenants such as telephone and data connections, mechanical, electrical, plumbing, and structural elements; floors, demising wall(s), sprinkler systems, fire alarms, interior insulation, storefront glass, and more.

The proposed scope of landlord work typically parallels the amount of tenant improvement dollars a tenant receives. If a landlord elects not to install a tenant's concrete floor or demising wall(s), the landlord will often provide a greater tenant improvement allowance to offset the increased construction cost a tenant must now pay to install these items.

There are times when a landlord will propose installing certain items that you should actually ask to install yourself if your landlord is willing to provide a higher TI allowance to offset the cost of taking on the work. Take restrooms: You likely don't know the desired location, size, or plumbing fixture layout of your restroom(s) when you're negotiating your LOI. If your landlord proposes to build a restroom with a single water closet (toilet) and lavatory (sink), but your eventual architect determines that because of your occupancy load you need two water closets in the restroom(s), you'll need to demolish part or all of the newly installed restroom. Or maybe after working with an architect you determine the restroom(s) would be better situated in a different area of your shop. Costs generally range from $10,000 to $22,500 per restroom, depending on the area in which you're building and the restroom's design, materials, and finishes.

Floors are a classic example. If you're going into a new shopping center that's still under construction, it's often best to take on the job of pouring your own floor (via your contractor). Why? Because if the landlord pours your floor, you'll need to pay a contractor to saw-cut and haul away the freshly poured concrete to install your underground plumbing and electrical, then pour fresh concrete over the newly installed plumbing and electrical work. In this case you'll save time and money by requesting an additional $4–$6 per square foot in tenant improvement dollars in exchange for pouring your own floor.

Consider having a consultant review the landlord work letter. A skilled consultant will review the work letter with the following in mind:

A) Review of missing or inaccurate landlord work-letter items that should be corrected or added to the landlord work letter

B) To determine any work-letter items that should be taken out of the landlord's scope of work in return for additional tenant improvement dollars

C) To review and appraise the value of typical landlord-provided construction items that are not included in the landlord work letter. If this dollar amount is higher than the proposed tenant improvement allowance, you have a bargaining chip with which to request an increase in your tenant improvement allowance.

## Noncompete Clauses

It's perfectly acceptable to request a noncompete clause (or exclusive-use clause) from your landlord. If the landlord accepts it, they would be barred from housing other tenants in the shopping center that fall under your noncompete description. For example, if you have a pizza shop, you could ask that no other food-service concept be allowed to sell pizza in the shopping center. If a noncompete barring pizza sales is too restrictive for the landlord because they want the ability to add, say, an "American eatery" that has various menu items, with pizza constituting a small portion of their sales, consider requiring a noncompete with wording such as *No other tenant is allowed to conduct business in the shopping center from which the sale of pizza derives 15 percent or more of its gross revenue over the course of a calendar quarter.*

Bear in mind, any noncompete is applicable only to your shopping center. Nothing prevents the landlord across the street from renting to a similar concept.

Some business owners believe "a rising tide lifts all boats" and prefer healthy competition and the spillover business a similar concept can garner. Noncompete agreements are not always in your interest. Consult with your broker or a consultant about your situation. Be wary: Some brokers oppose noncompetes because they restrict the pool of viable real estate, which lengthens the time it takes to close a deal.

### The Conflicting Interests of Tenants, Brokers, and Landlords

Many brokers have a high degree of integrity when working with clients, although it's important to understand that a broker's interest is not aligned with their client's. The more quickly a broker can get a tenant locked into a lease, the sooner they make their commission and move on to the next deal. Define the site attributes and metrics you believe necessary for success, and then hold true to those parameters. A seasoned broker may advise you to look at real estate that doesn't fit your metrics for good reason, but know when to put your foot down. Be a sponge. Absorb all advice, but at the end of the day, wring out the noise.

A broker is typically paid a commission by the landlord, based on the overall value of the deal. Your broker will make *twice* the commission on a 10-year rent period versus a 5-year deal. Higher rents and larger spaces also net brokers bigger paychecks. Don't get stuck in a space that's too expensive or larger than you need because someone else is telling you it's a good idea.

When a broker advises their client to push back on the landlord's requested square footage, rental rate, tenant improvement allowance amount, or lease period, they're negotiating against their own paycheck. As such, brokers don't have the incentives to haggle with a landlord for the best possible deal. Further, there's a decent chance the broker is already friends with the landlord, perhaps having worked with the landlord on previous deals. Or they're looking to work with the landlord on future deals and don't want to be known as a difficult broker.

This is where a consultant is of value. Consultants don't have the conflict of interest found with brokers. A good consultant knows how to push for the best possible lease terms by bending a landlord without breaking them. The extra $5–$10 per square foot in tenant improvement allowance or $1–$2 per square foot in lower rent that a skilled consultant can negotiate will result in tens of thousands of dollars in cost savings over the lifetime of a rental period. Consultants also provide nonbiased opinions on prospective real estate. Some brokers actually enjoy working with consultants, because it means less work for the broker to manage, review, and counteroffer LOI iterations and lease drafts.

To some degree there's a symbiotic relationship between landlords and tenants in which landlords succeed only when their tenants succeed. Ultimately landlords are looking for the best possible deal for themselves. Never feel pressured to continue with a deal that's soured. After spending months negotiating LOI and lease terms, becoming emotionally invested in the deal is inevitable. If a landlord switches you out of the agreed-upon space, increases rental costs, or changes your square footage, know when to speak up and be prepared to walk. It becomes easier to agree to a less favorable deal than what you originally started with after all the time and money spent on lease negotiations, but always hold true to your gut. Never enter into a lease you're not 100 percent comfortable with, for they say a commercial retail lease is a 10-year marriage, or till financial death do you part.

**Concept Brochure**

Provide landlords with a concept brochure so they can see what type of concept is really moving into their center. Without this, misconceptions can arise. Although you know you're a low-key beer-and-burger joint, a landlord may perceive you as a late-night, rowdy bar with loud music and the occasional parking lot fight. Or you know you're a professional therapeutic massage studio, but the landlord may believe your concept is a massage parlor that offers "special services"—not the tenant most landlords are looking for.

A landlord wants to know your industry numbers. Different industries have different success rates. Show the landlord why your concept's industry is a safe bet. Better yet, show the landlord why *you're* a safe bet so he'll be confident that you'll be able to pay rent for many years to come.

If you're with a franchise, highlight the franchise's system-wide success rate or other favorable franchise metrics. If you're an independent operator, talk up your former experience in your concept's industry. Landlords want to lease to people who have experience in their concept's industry or are members of a franchise that has a track record of success. These people are a much safer bet than people embarking on a "first-time science experiment."

A brochure shows you've got your stuff together. Securing great retail is cutthroat. Having a concept brochure gives you a leg up on the competing offer the landlord is entertaining. Be careful not to overdo it by boring the landlord with a research paper. Ten pages, slide-show style, with illustrative photos and concept bullet points, should do.

**Time Kills All Deals**

When you find a space you're interested in, get an LOI out to the landlord's representative immediately. Landlords are often slow to counter, routinely taking one to two weeks to respond to each LOI draft iteration. Don't play to their level. Send responses within 24 hours of getting a response from the landlord. Follow up with the landlord's agent after three or four days without response. Quick LOI responses and routine follow-ups show that you're serious about getting a deal done.

You never know what's happening behind the curtains. Unbeknownst to you, a landlord may be dragging her feet because she's working other deals, waiting for another deal to come in at full asking price, waiting for someone with better finances to come along, or looking for another offer to use as bargaining leverage. Regardless of the reason, slow negotiations are rarely for good cause.

Don't stoop to the landlord's slow response time. Not only does it leave an opening for a more attractive prospector to steal the deal, but it shows the landlord you're a slow mover during the easiest part of opening a store. If you're slow moving with real estate, how long will it take you to get through design, permitting, and construction? Landlords want spaces open ASAP. It adds property value, creates synergy within the shopping center, and makes other vacant spaces easier to lease.

It works both ways. A landlord may have been in LOI negotiations with another tenant, but your persistence and eagerness can be a show stealer!

Once a landlord issues a lease draft, odds become better that you'll secure the spot, but you're not out of the woods. There's always a potentially better deal out there for the landlord, so don't rest on your laurels.

Lack of quick responses by the landlord on lease draft iterations doesn't necessarily mean they're working other deals. Leases are a lot longer than LOIs and require an attorney's review. A landlord's lease response should take one to two weeks, but if the landlord has a busy attorney, the lease is long (50-plus pages), or the attorney is nitpicky with their review, a response can easily take two to four weeks. Regardless, be the squeaky wheel and keep the pressure up. Follow up with the landlord's broker after five business days without a response. Your follow-up increases their follow-through.

Conversely, if your attorney is the holdup, convey to the landlord that it's still under your team's review and you're eager to get the deal done. You never want a landlord to get cold feet or for them to think you're getting cold feet. Stay in constant communication.

## LOIs—Keep a Balance

The landlord community is a small one, and landlords talk among themselves. There's a decent chance the landlord's representative knows of other deals you're prospecting. If you blanket the town with LOIs, the landlord's agent will likely find out and turn a cold shoulder to your LOI. When you throw shit against the wall to see what sticks, it comes off as a lack of seriousness. A landlord's agent will ask himself, *Is this guy really interested in my space or am I just a backup deal to one of his six other LOIs? Why should I spend my time negotiating LOI terms when my odds of securing this tenant are slim?*

In other words, sending out too many LOIs damages your credibility. Keep outstanding LOIs to three deals maximum.

On the flip side, don't put all your eggs in one basket. Just as a landlord often talks to multiple prospects, it's okay to work two or three deals concurrently. If a deal falls through or sours, it's good to have another deal on the back burner to use as leverage or to fall back on, especially since LOI negotiations can take months.

## LOI Negotiations

The LOI negotiating process can be laborious, requiring multiple back-and-forth iterations of the LOI as the landlord and prospective tenant work through big-picture pre-lease terms. Work with your broker or consultant to determine how "hard" to negotiate. Every market and situation is different. You want to push for the best possible deal, although if you come in too aggressively on an initial offer, many landlords won't even counter. There are times when the rental rate should be accepted at full offering price, such as when you're in a tight real estate market where the landlord is entertaining multiple offers or the proposed rental rate is just a fair deal. With that said, take a broker's advice to not counter a rental rate with a grain of salt, because a broker's interest is to get a deal done, and the higher the deal value, the more money the broker makes.

Once both parties have agreed upon an LOI, the prospective tenant should sign and date the LOI, then forward it to the landlord and request a lease draft. Approximately half of landlords will countersign an LOI. The other half will simply send you a lease draft. Why don't landlords countersign LOIs? Because LOIs are *nonbinding*, meaning lease terms are subject to change. Although most leases hold true to the foundation of the LOI, things can change once a lease draft is issued.

**Lease Draft**

Both parties have agreed to an LOI, and the landlord has sent you a lease draft. At this point, you'll want to have a commercial lease attorney review *every* lease iteration on your behalf. If you've brought on a consultant, see if they'll do a cursory review.

Consultants and attorneys bring different sets of eyes to the review. Attorneys understand complex lease terminology and verbiage, and are able to spot discrepancies such as a plural word that should be singular in form. Commercial lease attorneys went to school for this. They're the professionals who understand legal terminology best and can catch the devil in the details.

Meanwhile, consultants are the people who work with clients up until a store's opening. They've seen many misfortunes caused by atypical, ambiguous, or unfavorable lease terms. The repetitive issues that a consultant sees are often unbeknownst to an attorney, who's rarely made aware of shortcomings after a lease is inked, which is when the issues come to light.

Once the tenant and landlord are satisfied with the lease verbiage, an executable copy will be issued for both parties to sign. Upon the signing of the lease (depending on the terms), the countdown to the rent-commencement date may start, so get started on your full set of architecture and engineering (A&E) plans immediately.

**Project Timeline**

It's important to be realistic about how long it will take to get your retail store open. Most people underestimate the time, and often by a long shot. I say this not as a deterrent but rather as a cautionary note so you can organize your finances and personal affairs accordingly. Quitting a job today and expecting your business to open in short order to provide income can become scary when you go longer than expected without money coming in the door.

It's no fun when you announce your anticipated opening date to the world, then chronically fail to meet deadlines—especially when you've told all your friends, your family, and the media! Creating media hype for an anticipated opening date four months down the road will fizzle out by the time you actually open 14 months from now. Don't get discouraged: Odds are, you're tracking just fine. Nothing worth having comes easily or quickly.

Like creating a budget, forecasting a development timeline is tough. Each stage of the process typically takes *much* longer than anticipated. Although there are those who have the fortune of opening their doors within a year of beginning the process (starting with the real estate hunt), many projects take more than a year, some more than two!

Case in point on the time to secure real estate: I analyzed 30 concepts that opened their doors between 2016 and 2018. All opened a restaurant, and all 30 had a professional real estate consultant assisting them. I reviewed only clients who ended up signing a lease. The median time to sign a lease from the day the client engaged with a broker was 239 days, or approximately eight months. Twelve operators (or 40 percent) signed a lease in less than six months. Eighteen (60 percent) took longer than six months.

Below is a generic high-level project timeline for a person looking to build a 2,500-square-foot coffee shop in a ready-to-go empty retail space. Bear in mind, timing will differ depending on the type of concept, the scope of work required, local market conditions, and the overall effort you put in. It's important to consider that being part of a well-polished franchise organization or hiring a consultant will generally speed up the process. Also note that this timeline does not factor in the conceptualization phase (creating a business plan) and assumes you're ready to hit the ground running with the real estate process.

*Real Estate Search and LOI Negotiations—4.5 months

Lease Negotiations—3 months

Architecture and Engineering—1.5 months

**Permitting and Acquiring a Contractor—2.5 months

GC Mobilization—.5 months

Construction—2.5 months

Hiring and Training—.5 months

-----------------------------------

**OPEN FOR BUSINESS 15 MONTHS LATER**

*The time to find real estate varies drastically. Some people spend months trying to negotiate LOIs on multiple locations that fall through. Others are successful in executing an LOI and signing a lease on the first location they submit an LOI on. Successfully negotiating a single LOI should take no more than 45 days.

**The time to acquire a building permit varies drastically, depending on economic conditions and where you're building. Some owners receive their building permit in four weeks, others not for over a year. Generally speaking, it's easier and quicker to get building permits in small cities.

When the economy is strong, there's an increase in building permit applications for a finite number of city plan reviewers to sort through and review, increasing the overall time it takes to receive building permits.

**Site Survey**

A site survey can be likened to a home inspection on a commercial space. It's used to determine the existing location and condition of building attributes such as architectural, mechanical, electrical, plumbing, civil, and structural conditions. A surveyor will take photos and laser measurements, and document existing site attributes using computer-aided design (CAD) software. If requested, the surveyor can produce a report documenting items that may need to be replaced or upgraded or are missing altogether. Your eventual architect or design professional will then use the site survey files to produce a set of construction drawings with accurate plan measurements based on the surveyor's CAD file.

Some franchise and corporate organizations require that every prospective retail space be surveyed before locking into a lease. Others survey only older spaces with little or no space documentation available. As a general rule of thumb, the following spaces should be strongly considered for a site survey *before* lease execution:

1. Any location in a multistory building where there are building elements above or below the space, such as parking garages below or apartments above

2. Any space that's second-generation or older (where previous tenants have occupied the space)
3. It's prudent to survey new construction (where the shell building is already built). New construction is not immune to discrepancies between the shell plans and actual "as-built" site conditions. I've surveyed new construction where there were multiple mismatches between the fresh shell plans and actual "as-built" conditions.

Having a site survey performed is your best bet to hedge against inaccuracies with your construction drawings (which will cause problems down the road during construction). In lieu of having a site survey performed, the following items will aid in an architect's ability to produce your store's plans:

1. The full set of original .PDF "as-built" shell construction drawings
2. The latest full set of "as-built" tenant improvement construction drawings (if the space is second generation or older)
3. The base floor plan in CAD format
4. Site photos and videos of the interior space, exterior of the building, fire riser room, electrical room, and roof

In addition to the time and money saved by designing and building off accurate survey files, a site survey can save time and build-out cost by illustrating existing building elements that the architect or design professional can incorporate into your store's floor plan. For example, if the water inlet line and sanitary sewage line are on the right-hand side of your space, an architect would design plumbing elements such as restrooms to go on that side.

Conversely, if you're going into a second-generation space with existing interior walls or fixtures left over by a previous tenant, your architect will try to reuse and reincorporate as many existing site attributes and mechanical, electrical, or plumbing systems as possible.

A site survey may reveal that systems are missing or insufficient for your store's use. You can then determine whether the time and cost required to upgrade or add new services or systems is worthwhile. This gives you the ability to back out of a deal *before* locking into a lease. Conversely, survey results can be used as leverage to request additional tenant improvement allowances from the landlord.

Depending on the size of a space, its current condition, how quickly you need a site survey completed, and the scope of survey work to be performed, site surveys for retail spaces generally cost between $1,000 and $3,500. The typical time to complete a site survey is two to three weeks from the day you contract with the surveyor, because they will need to schedule a survey date, then spend time buttoning up their CAD files and writing a report before issuing it. I've been able to fly out to a job site, survey a space, then issue a report within three days of a client's request, but that's tough to do. Plan ahead so that a site survey is not holding up the signing of your lease.

If you choose to survey a space, coordinate with the landlord's representative to make sure the surveyor has access to all needed areas during the day of the survey. This typically includes the interior space, fire riser room, electrical room (if different from the fire riser room), IT room, and rooftop. Failure to provide full site access to the surveyor will result in a partial survey or overtime cost as the surveyor waits for a property manager to provide access. At $100 to $200 an hour in overtime cost, it adds up quickly.

A quick internet search for "retail site survey" will net many results. If you're bringing on a consultant who's proficient in CAD with experience in surveying spaces, consider having them perform the survey. It keeps accountability all under one roof and allows the consultant to have early and intimate familiarity with your space—a big bonus, since they'll be assisting with your store's design and construction. Many architects can also survey spaces. If you already know which architect you're using, consider having them perform the survey. Be cautious about having general contractors perform surveys. They're generally not as thorough, and often don't use AutoCAD or Revit software, which are the industry-standard CAD software programs that design professionals use and that should be used to perform your survey.

**Project Management**

Throughout the development of your store, make sure you're expedient in completing tasks. The squeaky wheel gets the grease, and it certainly leads to a quicker opening. Be in constant contact with your real estate, design, equipment, and construction partners to keep them on track and relay all applicable information among the appropriate parties. Make sure you have all the right players lined up *ahead* of time.

Unless you hire a consultant, *you* will need to be the squeaky wheel, project orchestrator, and distributor of information. Always request deadlines for cost proposals and the completion of work. Send follow-up emails or phone calls after 24–72 hours of no response. *Your follow-up increases their follow-through*. If architectural plans are due in three weeks, it doesn't hurt to send an email a week and a half before they're due with a polite reminder of the due date and the urgency of meeting deadlines. Although this is your only project, it's one of many projects your architect or contractor is working on. When you don't follow up, it's easy for them to forget or to push your project off when they have another client who's caught their ear. Time is money. Be the bull and clear your own path.

Don't let any landlord-provided free-rent period slow your store's development. That 90–150-day free-rent period is usually used up before you're open. Let's say your rent is $10,000 a month. That's $333 out the door in rent for every day you're not open. The total losses are probably closer to $400 to $500 a day when you factor in all costs: loan interest, common-area maintenance costs, accounting, monthly software and business fees, pre-open insurance, employees already hired... The list can get long.

Your losses are actually greater than $400 to $500 a day, because a wise business owner looks at the totality of the situation. You're not in business to pay your bills and break even. You've invested your time and money in a concept because you believe it can be profitable. What's the lost potential profit for every day your doors aren't open? $150? $1,000? When you add it up, the net difference to your bank account is sobering. How much collective time was lost while you waited an extra 24 hours to answer that email, return a phone call, resolve that contractor dispute, or finalize design details? Slow communication often results in weeks or months in collective delays and causes significant sway in your bank account down the road. Most new business owners have tight budgets and can't afford these self-destructive delays.

Pro tip: Figure out the financial impact for every day you're not open. Remember that number and use it as motivation to expeditiously knock out tasks.

# PART 3: DESIGN AND ARCHITECTURE

**The Role of an Architect**

An architect produces your store's floor plan and all additional plan documents needed to get building permits and construct your store. To make this happen, architects will facilitate or make recommendations on furniture, fixtures, equipment, finishes, and design options. Architects will bring engineers on board to produce certain engineering drawings. After plans have been completed, architects will work through plan review comments from pesky city officials, and they'll answer technical questions posed by general contractors. Some architects will even help with construction management. Architects can also assist during the real estate selection process by advising on code considerations, design questions, and mechanical, electrical, and plumbing requirements.

We often talk of architects as if they're the singular force in producing a business's plans. In reality it is typical for draftsmen to work under architects. There are also multiple engineers who produce mechanical, electrical, plumbing, and structural drawings. Ultimately the architect is the master orchestrator of all the design professionals. The flow of communications typically goes through the architect.

There are architecture firms and engineering firms, but they're not commonly combined. This means architects must sub out the engineering work to third-party firms.

Luckily a good architect does this seamlessly, with the client rarely hassled or even informed about the different design companies involved in the production of their store's plans. Architects will get quotes from engineering firms and then include engineering costs in their client's architecture proposal so the client is contracting with and paying only one entity: the architect.

**When to Bring an Architect On Board**

A costly mistake new business owners often make involves getting an architect on board after they've signed a lease. That's too late! Find an architect when you start your real estate search. Why? An architect can assist with site attribute questions or address potential code issues *before* you lock into a lease. Equally as important, they'll be able to produce a floor plan on the space before you've secured your real estate. After producing a floor plan, you just might find the space to be too small or narrow to be operationally sufficient. That's not a mistake you want to make after signing a lease.

An architect is the standard avenue of plan production. You could use a contractor, but that's not advised (see "Design-Build" below).

If you're in a franchise organization, you may have the option of using a national preferred architect or finding a local architect. I typically favor using the franchisor's architect. They can produce plans faster than a one-off architect because they're site-adapting prototypical drawings, not starting from scratch. Further, their familiarity with the concept and its many nuances should mean fewer mistakes and quicker plan production when drafting additional franchise store plans.

## Finding an Architect

Get an architect who specializes in retail tenant improvement work. Using an architect who primarily does residential housing, core and shell work, commercial office space, or other nonretail market segments is not advised. Not sure what their area of expertise is? Check their website. A firm's online project portfolio is typically a good representation of their area of expertise.

Food-service concepts in particular present a level of sophistication and challenge on the design side (versus traditional retail), given the nuances surrounding the bar and kitchen, cooking hoods, health code considerations, and subtle equipment considerations. If you're planning to build a restaurant or bar, work with a design professional who's well polished in the market segment.

If you're looking for a food-service architect, consider Design Parameters. An architecture firm with offices in Dallas and Denver, they specialize in restaurants and bars. Design Parameters has built food-service concepts in darn near every corner of the country for franchises and independent operators alike. Their industry knowledge, level of plan detail, and ability to follow through has made them my go-to recommendation for food-service clients. They're not always the cheapest, but the age-old adage "You get what you pay for" certainly rings true.

https://www.designparameters.com

inquiry@designparameters.com

People often recommend using a local architect, claiming that local design professionals know the code better than out-of-state architects. This is largely unfounded advice. Although code can differ from city to city, and state to state, it's often not by much, and everyone is adhering to the International Building Code (IBC) framework, just with local deviations in some instances. Any local code amendments are easily accessible for out-of-towners to review. Since you're darn near guaranteed to receive city plan review comments (see "Permitting" section), any local code items are typically addressed by the plan reviewer and architect during the permitting stage (before the commencement of construction).

There are drawbacks to using architects from out of town. They're not able to visit the job site or perform site surveys without travel costs. Nor can they log plans into cities that still require physical plan submittals. These drawbacks aren't typically deal breakers, as there are workarounds such as using local firms that specialize in site surveys or running plans down to the city yourself.

**Floor Plan**

New business owners tend to discount just how much dining room or retail sales space they'll have after accounting for all auxiliary store components. Hallways, restrooms, and walkways must be kept to minimum distances for emergency egress and Americans with Disabilities Act (ADA) code clearances. For instances, ADA code requires that certain areas maintain a 60-inch wheelchair-turn radius. The need for additional egress doors, hallways, wheelchair ramps, vestibules, or extra restrooms are design elements that may be required in your floor plan that you likely didn't consider when you made a napkin sketch of your store. These items can quickly eat into the overall square footage of your concept, reducing allowable retail sales space.

It's devastating when an owner locks into a lease and tells the architect she needs a minimum of 900 square feet of retail sales space for her art gallery to make the numbers pencil out, but after accounting for all code variables, the architect is able to produce only 400 square feet of retail space.

Restaurant owners are notorious for underestimating how many seats their space can hold. Ever been to a sit-down restaurant and wondered how the place makes their numbers work with just 15 seats and little to-go business? Odds are decent the owner envisioned a much larger dining room but didn't realize how much space a kitchen takes up or that he'd need two bathrooms and an additional egress door, all of which was uncovered after he signed a lease and found an architect.

Avoid the *Oh, shit: This place is too small. What have I done?* moment by having an architect produce a preliminary floor plan before you're too far down the road with real estate negotiations.

Architects often charge $500–$2,500 for a floor-plan drawing. In the event that letter-of-intent or lease negotiations fall through, you'll be out of pocket for most of the floor-plan cost since the work is largely nontransferable from one location to the next, but that's a necessary risk worth taking.

A floor plan is a concepts layout. It's a single-page drawing indicating the placement of critical concept elements such as interior walls, electrical panels, furniture, and equipment.

Your architect can advise you about which shopping center plans they need to produce your store's plans and the format they need to be in. The architect typically needs a copy of any site survey you've had performed, as well as certain landlord's shell plans. Refer to "Site Survey," in part 2, for the plans likely needed.

Architects generally include costs for two or three versions of a floor plan. Requesting more floor-plan iterations than what's specified in your architect's contract will incur additional cost. Don't be afraid to request additional floor plans or tweaks if you're not fully satisfied with what's been proposed, because once you've selected a floor plan and released the architect to produce your full set of plans, changes cost a lot more money and time.

If you request a revised location of the bathrooms when deciding on a floor plan, that change is relatively straightforward, requiring the architect to make changes to just the one-page floor plan. If you ask to move the restrooms after the full set of plans has been produced, a ripple effect of changes will be required on virtually every plan page, which could include reflective-ceiling plans, framing-and-slab plans, equipment plans, and elevation plans, as well as every page of mechanical, electrical, and plumbing plans.

If substantial plan changes are made, and assuming the plans have already been submitted to the city for building permits, you'll need to file for a plan amendment that illustrates the changes. This typically results in delays to acquire your building permits, because plan reviewers must review your plans an additional time.

## Plans (Construction Documents)

Once you've finalized a floor plan, you'll need to determine when to release the architect to produce all the supporting plan pages. Plans are pictures, drawings, diagrams, and verbiage outlining how your store will be constructed. Before you can build your business, design professionals need to put your concept onto paper.

Once plans have been drawn up, they must be sent to the city for review. After the city is satisfied that the plans meet code compliance, building permits will be issued.

You'll also need plans so contractors can provide accurate pricing, and of course, the contractor will need plans to know how to build your store.

Collectively, full sets of plans are called many things: plans, construction documents, CDs, drawings, construction drawings, TI (tenant improvement) plans, prints, blueprints, A&E plans... It can get confusing. For the purposes of this book, we'll try to stick to *plans* or *construction documents*.

## Producing Plans Pre-Lease

Assuming you don't have a signed lease but you've finalized a floor plan, be cautious about releasing the architect and their engineers to produce your plans. Without a signed lease, you haven't secured the retail space. If the architect produces plans on the space, and eleventh-hour lease negotiations fall through, your plans are not transferable to another space. This means you'll be on the hook to pay the architect and engineers for their time spent drawing plans on your current space.

That said, I'd estimate 70–75 percent of lease negotiations come to fruition once a lease draft has been sent to the client. Going ahead and getting plans completed while you're negotiating the lease is one of the best ways to speed up your development timeline.

Most store owners pay at least one to two months' worth of dark rent. Therefore, getting plans started before you've secured the space will likely save money down the road—assuming the landlord turnover-to-tenant date is based on the execution of your lease and not the date your building permit is received. The latter typically affords you more time to build your store without paying too much, or any, dark rent.

Of course, if lease negotiations fall through and you've got a set of plans on a space that's not yours, you could be out big bucks. Ultimately it's a business decision that only you can make.

If you release your architect to produce plans early, consider waiting until the landlord has provided their first iteration of lease comments, and make sure they're favorable. Favorable first-round lease comments increase your odds of executing a lease.

Starting a business is about taking risk. There's no certainty of success in business, but it's a measured risk you believe to be worthwhile. The time-value and payoff of having plans completed early is a risk you should consider, but always go with your gut.

**Plan Production Time**

The time for architects and engineers to complete plans varies drastically based on the scope of work needed, level of plan detail desired by the client, timing for an owner to nail down finishes and furniture, fixtures, and equipment (FF&E), the architect's current workload, and whether you're a one-off store or replicated franchise concept.

For a one-off store, completion of plans should take 4–12 weeks. Franchise plans are often completed in just 2–4 weeks. Communicate expectations for the architect and engineers' time to complete your plans when you're reviewing the architect's contract so that everyone's on the same page.

The best way to keep your architect on track is to periodically reach out while they're drawing your plans. It doesn't hurt to relay the urgency of completing plans on time to avoid paying dark rent or penalties to the landlord for not having plans completed within 30 to 90 days of signing the lease (a stipulation some landlords require). Bear in mind, your architect is working with many clients. The occasional reach-out will help ensure your project is top of mind. The squeaky wheel gets the grease!

Your architect will occasionally reach out while creating your plans as questions or issues come up. Be quick in responding to them! Ten emails that each take two days to respond to can cause significant delays in the completion of your plans. These are unnecessary self-inflicted wounds!

**Food-Service Floor Plans**

Designing a food-service concept often starts with the kitchen layout. Hallways, restrooms, and the dining room will key off the kitchen. For a design professional to lay out your kitchen, they'll need an equipment list. Your food-and-drink menu dictates the equipment list. Some architects can produce an equipment list based on a store's menu, but many can't. That's where a kitchen equipment contractor (KEC) comes in. A good KEC has extensive knowledge of kitchen equipment and can even design your kitchen (and bar). If a KEC designs your kitchen, the architect will review it for code compliance, then incorporate the KEC drawing into your overall floor-plan drawing.

There are some great KECs with kitchen designers who are former chefs. Their knowledge about equipment and their expertise in kitchen design and operational flow can add serious value!

The take-home point? You'll need to have your food-and-drink menu largely solidified before working with an architect. If you don't know everything that will be served, ask the architect or KEC to provide a little extra free space. It's easier to design for expansionary measures now than to try to fit a square peg into a round hole later.

**Design-Build**

Although architects are the most common avenue for producing plans, there's another option: "design-build" plans. Doing a design-build entails having a general contractor and his subcontractors produce your store's plans. In many cases, architects and engineers must review or assist in plan production, as well as take liability for or stamp the plans, but it's ultimately the GC's brainchild.

If you've never had a general contractor build a store for you, design-build is not the advised route to go. Why? A GC will often add the stipulation of being the first or often the only GC to bid the project. Design-build projects are an alluring option for new store owners because contractors may promise to complete your plans for "free" or for a heavily discounted fee. In actuality, the cost is wrapped into the GC's construction bid. In some instances, you'll actually pay *more* for design-build plans, because contractors' bids are generally higher when there's no competition.

Another design-build cautionary note: During construction it can be harder to verify the validity of problems and change orders when the designer and builder are one and the same.

The adage "You get what you pay for" often rings true with design-build plans as well. Architects and engineers have extensive knowledge and background in design and plan production. Contractors don't. A little-known fact is that architects and engineers typically go to school for as long as doctors before they're fully licensed and able to stamp their signature on a set of plans. The systems they design can be technical in nature. Their years of schooling teach them the rhyme and reason for using certain design materials or systems and avoiding others. Builders haven't been through the same education as architects and engineers, and they don't always fully understand the systems they're installing or the potential disadvantages of substituting certain design materials.

Some GCs make it appear that they have an in-house architect producing their design-build plans since they may advertise the ability to produce "architectural plans." Unless their draftsman has the credentials of a registered architect (RA), they're not an architect. The best way to find out if someone is a licensed architect is to do a web search or call your state board of architects. A person cannot represent themselves as an architect unless they are licensed to do work in your particular state. Calling oneself an architect without the proper licensure in the state where the work is performed is illegal.

Many architects belong to organizations such as the following:

- AIA (American Institute of Architects)
- ALA (Association of Licensed Architects)

Membership in these organizations does not automatically mean that person is an architect. Industry professionals who are not architects such as consultants and contractors can also belong to these groups.

## Plan Costs

A loose rule of thumb is that plans should cost approximately 8 percent of the value of construction. Of this, 4–5 percent is paid to the architect, with the balance going to the engineers. This rule of thumb doesn't always hold true. In fact, I see A&E costs vary significantly, running anywhere from $5,000 to $70,000, depending on the scope of work requested, level of drawing detail desired, size of the space, and type of concept.

This is a bit outside the scope of this book, but if you're doing "ground-up" construction (turning a plot of dirt into a building), you'll also pay for surveying, civil engineering, structural engineering, and landscape plans. Costs for plans on an empty "shell" or building can cost $40,000 to $120,000 or more. That's on top of the $5,000–$70,000 for your tenant improvement plans.

Communicate your construction budget to your architect. It's their job to attempt to design your store to meet your budget. I say *attempt*, because knowing the actual construction cost before you've received bids from general contractors is very difficult. Nonetheless, based on your budget, many architects can determine whether they need to design to the bare minimum for your store's finishes and materials or if there's some flexibility. Architects would rather specify high-quality materials and systems that will last 8 to 10-plus years, but if you're on a shoestring budget, that may not be possible.

An architect should be able to give guidance on whether your budget is even realistic. You'll be hard-pressed to find any retail concept over 1,000 to 1,500 square feet that can be built for less than $50,000. Many can't even be built for $100,000 to $150,000.

Unlike a general contractor, architects typically get paid a fixed dollar amount, not a sum based on a percentage of the construction cost. Therefore, there's no motivation for architects to inflate your design and material costs to make the project more expensive. On the off chance they request payment based on the value of construction, proceed with caution!

**Franchise Plans**

Using a franchisor's national architect is typically cheaper than working with a one-off architect, because the national architect is largely site-adapting prototypical drawings, not starting from scratch. Further, their pricing is likely prenegotiated with the franchisor based on doing multiple projects. And of course, the second time is always quicker. Since time is money, this means cheaper plan costs.

If you're in a franchise organization, the franchisor may lead the charge on design, requiring architects to design your store to certain corporate design standards. Depending on the franchise, you may have a wide degree of flexibility with design or next to none. Generally speaking, newer franchises provide more design leniency to franchisees than established brands. Established brands that have built many stores often have a rhyme and reason for even the most minute of store design details, having learned what works and what doesn't from previous stores. Take their considerations seriously (assuming you have a say).

Ask your franchisor how much say you have on your store's layout, finishes, and equipment options. Your franchise may have had a design package with beautiful overhead trellises or a fancy millwork package that was taken out of the concept's design to keep build-out costs low. Why? Franchises constantly review opening project costs and often strip out or substitute cheaper design materials to keep their franchise disclosure document (FDD) costs low. The lower the opening store cost listed in their FDD, the more franchise contracts a franchisor will sell. Ask your franchisor if you can consider incorporating additional design elements into your store's design if you'd like to have more options.

## Interior Design

Some people prefer to hire an interior designer (ID) to advise on the selection of finishes, décor, and design elements. An interior designer is not used in lieu of an architect, but rather in addition to one. Architects generally do a fine job on design, but an interior designer is a design specialist. Interior design is not an architect's main objective, because they're also tasked with conforming to energy, fire, health, life safety, practicality, and usable clearance codes, as well as incorporating engineering drawings into their plans.

Some IDs spend 10–20 hours selecting design elements, and others spend 60-plus, all the while going over the most minute of lighting and door-handle details. Interior designers charge anywhere from $50 to $200 an hour. Some architecture firms have a dedicated ID on staff.

A good ID has exemplary knowledge of design elements and the ability to provide unmatched insight into items such as sound abatement, lighting, and first-impression appearances; most architects can only scratch the surface when it comes to helping with those considerations.

Provide the ID with descriptive words and images you hope your business will evoke. The interior designer can bring those words to life, whether you want your store's design and décor to give off a warm, earthy, or modern-luxury feeling, or even a blend of the three.

Convey your budget from the start. Nothing's worse than spending a great deal of time and money producing something beautiful, only to find out during the construction bid process that it's too expensive. At that point you'll have to pay your interior designer *more* money to conform to your budget.

Like artists, no two interior designers are the same. Everyone has a slightly different design style. They also have different areas of expertise—such as residential versus commercial. If you choose to bring an ID on board, look through their online project portfolio to see if their project type and design styles match your preferences. Can't find someone who shares your design preference? Surely you've been in a business whose design resonated with you, evoking the style you've envisioned for your store. If so, they likely used a professional designer (or possibly just a multitalented architect). Ask the business owner whom they used.

Ready to hire an ID, but not sure if their value-add is worth it? Ask a couple of softball questions on different material cost points and durability. A good ID can rattle off a multitude of flooring materials, with knowledge about price points, product maintenance, and longevity. Consider using a local ID who can provide material boards that you can touch and feel. A local ID also allows you to tour the town with them, experiencing real-world examples that inspire.

If you're going to use an interior designer, let your architect know before contracting with either the ID *or* the architect. Set up an "introduction" call in which you, the architect, and the ID discuss everyone's roles. This builds team synergy, prevents confusion about both professionals' project responsibilities, and can avoid additional costs that the architect may have assumed was their responsibility.

The architect and ID will need to identify how to incorporate each other's work. Do they both use AutoCAD or Revit? If so, can the architect send their working CAD drawings to the ID to edit? Does the ID use a different program, requiring the architect to provide blank plan pages for the ID to mark up using a .PDF editor? Is the ID only selecting design materials, then expecting the architect to do all the drawing legwork? Who's creating the materials list? When does the architect need the interior designer's documents so they can submit plans to the city on time? Having an "introduction" call will answer these questions and better assure the successful production of your business's construction documents.

Of course, you certainly don't have to use an ID. Many people handle the task themselves or work in concert with their architect. In fact, many architects are happy to take on the interior design work. Everyone has their strong suits, so do your due diligence.

When deciding whether to use an ID, consider the time value they bring. They're spending the time to source materials and design elements. They also know what materials are better from a cost and durability standpoint. There's no business return on the three weeks you spent researching and selecting design materials. Those three weeks of DIY designing only detracted from the three weeks you could've spent working on marketing or operational materials to grow your business.

**Owner Versus GC Responsibility to Furnish and Install**

When you're working with your design professionals to create plans, you'll need to determine who's responsible for furnishing (providing) and installing everything. If the plans do not indicate who's furnishing and installing unmarked construction items, it's generally assumed the GC is responsible for furnishing and installing them. As such, an architect may not define the responsibility of who will provide construction materials such as framing and drywall. Although almost everything *could* be provided by the owner (with GC installation), most fixed-in-place construction items are provided by the contractor. With that said, flooring, lighting, millwork, and plumbing fixtures are examples of construction materials that owners sometimes provide.

Although construction materials are generally assumed to be contractor provided and installed, equipment, furniture, and IT components (low-voltage data, and audio and security systems) are generally assumed to be owner provided and installed.

Knowing which party is providing all the various materials and equipment can be confusing, but you *must* ensure that you and the contractor know exactly who's providing what to avoid headaches and project delays.

If you wish to provide certain construction materials, let the architect know so that they can mark up the plans accordingly. Why do some owners take on the responsibility of providing certain construction materials? Because subcontractors typically add a 10 percent markup to supply materials, and then the general contractor will tag on their overhead and profit (typically 7–13 percent), making the overall markup approximately 17–23 percent.

"My God, I should supply all the construction materials myself!" you exclaim.

Not so fast. Contractors and their subs generally get big material price breaks because of their large purchase levels. An electrician can easily get 50 percent (or more) off a lighting fixture's list price.

Further, owners often discount the time and effort it takes to supply materials. There's price shopping, lead times, payments, and facilitating the delivery. When items arrive broken, missing, incomplete, or late, the purchaser is the one dealing with the headaches.

Something as simple as providing the lighting package can be a learning curve for first-timers. How much pendant down-rod do you need? Incandescent or LED fixtures? Type of bulbs? Canopy needed? Canopy color? Baffle color? Shade or no shade? The takeaway: Consider leaving construction materials to the GC to source. You've got enough on your plate!

### Sound Abatement

When designing a retail or food-service concept, attention to the acoustics is often nonexistent. If you're opening a retail space with loud equipment or flocks of patrons constantly conversing, you've likely got a noisy concept on your hands. Designing for sound abatement today is easier than fixing it once it becomes a problem and you've lost customers.

How many times have you been in a restaurant where you can't hear what another person is saying at a normal tone? Or been to a workout studio with echoing equipment that interrupts your ability to listen to your music or listen to the workout instructor?

Not only is a loud business unpleasant, but it can be costly, particularly for food-service establishments. Some customers won't return to a restaurant because they had a hard time hearing their friend over dinner. Also think of all the orders taken incorrectly by waiters or bartenders unable to hear what customers order. Noise is one of the main reasons for wrong restaurant orders.

The design trends of yesteryear—floor carpeting and table spreads—have been swapped for today's trendy finishes of brick, concrete, tile, glass, and wood. Although practical from a cleanliness standpoint (easy to wipe down), and a popular choice of architects, these hard surfaces make for lots of sound reverberation and a loud room!

To reduce sound, you need to reduce echo and reverberation by adding surfaces with an absorptive material. One of the most effective sound-reducing methods is the installation of acoustic panels. If you have an open ceiling (meaning the building's trusses and roof are visible) or a ceiling made of hard materials, consider adding acoustic panels throughout the ceiling of the retail sales floor or dining room, where noise is commonly an issue. I've found little difference in the effectiveness of vertically versus horizontally hung acoustic panels. Both methods work well. If you have high ceilings (more than about 20 feet), consider placing the panels lower for better results. Be mindful of existing conditions such as sprinkler heads and HVAC diffusers that may need to be rerouted after acoustic panels are installed.

Sound abatement panels are made from different materials. Solid foam, wood fiber strands, and cloth-wrapped frames are common. Good acoustic panels are not cheap, nor are installation costs (it can take a two-man crew one to two days). Depending on your area, the material used, and site conditions, installing 15 sound panels that are 1 inch thick by 4 feet wide by 8 feet long to the upper deck of your store can cost $4,000 to $16,000.

In addition to the ceiling, consider putting sound-abatement panels on interior walls. Worried they won't be aesthetically pleasing? You can kill two birds with one stone by printing high-quality graphics on sound panels to be used as wall artwork or marketing material. An internet search will bring up many companies that can imprint high-resolution graphics on sound panels.

Installing sound-abatement panels on the walls and ceiling will significantly reduce sound levels to an acceptable volume for most concepts. If you really want to deafen the noise, consider installing sound-absorbing flooring such as carpet or a large rug. You can also get window drapes or use a spray-on acoustic fiber on gypsum walls (drywall). Chairs with seat cushions and padded backs made of porous material such as cloth will also help (leather not so much).

Those on a budget can consider forming an alliance with a local artist. It's free to you, keeps your decor constantly updated, and provides exposure for the artist. It can mean a slight bump in business as the artist, their followers, or artistic community members patronize your store. Many artists even pay a 5–20 percent commission to store owners for showcasing and facilitating the sale of their artwork. What a win-win all around! When hanging artwork for soundproofing purposes, use open-weave artwork painted on cloth or canvas. Note that this method of sound abatement is less effective than acoustic panels or carpet since the paint is a barrier, blocking some of the sound absorption. Regardless, I've worked with store owners who've seen a mitigation in sound levels after installing artwork in their stores.

All that said, you don't want to make your business too quiet. After all, proper sound levels exude energy and liveliness. Also note that adding padding to the underside of tables and chairs will provide minimal sound abatement and makes cleaning gum off a table's underside challenging.

If you know your store will have loud noises or a herd of talkative patrons, designing for sound abatement is not difficult and can increase business. You can do it yourself without hiring a sound engineer!

**Soundproofing**

If you're a concept such as a doctor's office or massage studio, you should be cognizant of reducing or silencing the volume of external noises such as street traffic and neighboring tenants.

If you're going into a standalone space, you'll probably be okay. For the rest of us in shopping centers, knowing that your next-door neighbor is a quiet concept is not always enough. Why? Because neighboring tenants change all the time. That 30-year-old furniture store that you share a demising wall with could be gone tomorrow, replaced with a noisy restaurant.

I ran into such a situation recently. A massage studio owner was worried that the only thing between their business and my client's kitchen (which had loud music and clunking pots and pans) was a 6-inch demising wall that was not soundproofed. The massage studio failed to soundproof their walls during their TI work, and instead requested that my client carry the burden.

Although the massage studio agreed to pay the cost for us to soundproof, they asked us to add additional framing and specialty drywall that would impede an additional 5 to 6 inches into our space. Along with the lost usable space, the 5 to 6 inches would've created a ripple effect of floor-plan changes, requiring a readjustment to multiple construction document pages, including architectural, mechanical, electrical, and plumbing layouts.

We ended up installing an additional 5/8-inch section of drywall with a soundproofing joint compound. It wasn't what the massage studio wanted, but my client decided the time and cost impact was not worth his headaches.

The takeaway from this? You never know with certainty who your neighbor will be a year from now. If your concept requires quiet from exterior noises, it's best to plan now as opposed to trying to soundproof later or hoping that others will accommodate your wishes. As the old saying goes, "A lack of planning on your part doesn't constitute an emergency on mine."

So how do you soundproof? There's a myriad of options. I'll run through the heavy hitters.

1.  **Doors**—If you're trying to soundproof a particular room, buy a soundproof door. These can be expensive, so if cost is top of mind, consider a solid-core door. Solid-core doors are leaps and bound better at blocking noise than their hollow-core counterparts. Keep air gaps to no more than ¼ inch. Install soundproofing rubber around the door frame before adding molding. Finally, consider installing an automatic door bottom to the underside of the door. This allows for a hermetic seal unsurpassed by even the best door sweeps.

2.  **Walls**—Generally speaking, the denser and thicker a wall, the more sound resistant it becomes, since sound waves are slowed by mass. Brick, concrete masonry units (CMU), and solid-pour concrete walls are significantly better at blocking sound than their drywall counterpart. The downside to these walls? They require more cost and time to construct. Although they're great at blocking exterior noises, they're a hard surface, which causes interior volumes to increase since sound bounces off their face rather than being absorbed.

3.  **Soundproof drywall**—Demising walls and interior walls built from wooden studs or light-gauge metal

studs encased in drywall are the most common types of retail walls. They're cost efficient and quick to build. Drywall is a panel made of gypsum, fibrous materials, and a glue-like adhesive binding it together with paper on the exterior of the drywall. Drywall composites differ, depending on their application—general use, soundproof, moisture, mold, or fire resistant. Soundproof drywall has added layers of gypsum and paper along with a viscoelastic and ceramic core that blocks incoming sound waves. Depending on the manufacture and the thickness of soundproof drywall used (typically 5/8 inch for commercial spaces), a single sheet of soundproof drywall is claimed to block as much noise as eight sheets of regular drywall stacked on top of each other. Bear in mind, soundproof drywall costs three to six times more than standard drywall. Granted, traditional drywall is dirt cheap, and regardless of the drywall used, the install cost should be the same.

4. **Soundproof joint compound**—Standard drywall joint compound or "mud" goes between sheets of drywall. The problem with joint compound is that it cracks over time. Cracks let in noise. There are soundproofing joint compounds such as Green Glue that are not rigid like normal joint compounds; rather, they're rubbery and elastic, providing an acoustic sound barrier to noise. These sealants are made to fill gaps between edges, joints, and seams of drywall, and are not meant to

go over the drywall. Soundproofing joint compounds are easy to use and cost-effective.

5. **Insulation**—The cheapest soundproofing? Insulation! Energy code requirements dictate that a building's envelope be insulated to a certain R-value. R-values are metrics that determine the effectiveness of insulation. The higher the R-value, the greater the effectiveness. Most modern buildings are required to be insulated in both the walls and ceilings to certain R-values based on the type of construction and their geographic location. If your space happens not to be insulated, ask the landlord how they passed their energy International Energy Conservation Code Comcheck report. It's typically the landlord's responsibility to insulate a building's envelope to conform to local energy code before leasing the space.

Noisy neighbor above you? Add insulation! Depending on the severity of the noise, you may also have to use soundproof drywall.

What's an unintended by-product of soundproofing? Energy savings! There's a parallel between soundproofing and energy efficiency. Just as sound travels through gaps in a building's envelope, so does air. Blocking air also blocks sound.

### Low-Voltage Data

The ball often gets dropped for low-voltage installation, so let's make sure you've got a game plan in place. Low voltage is data cable wiring connected to outlets so you can plug in and run equipment such as Wi-Fi routers, speakers, security systems, fax machines, televisions, computers, point-of-sale (POS) systems, and telephones.

Contractors usually exclude install of low voltage. Many architects also exclude drawing low-voltage plans from their scope of work. If the architect is able to provide these plans, I prefer that they do so. Although it will likely cost an extra $500–$1,500, it can save time and money in the long run. How? By completing the wiring plan early, you won't be scrambling to find a vendor who can produce their own drawings and complete the install on time. Also, when you have a set of low-voltage plans from an architect, you can shop them to multiple vendors for quotes. Prices vary, so consider shopping the job to two or three vendors. If your architect won't create a low-voltage plan, you'll need to work directly with a low-voltage data cabling company. Going this route doesn't allow you to shop the plans to multiple vendors.

Whoever produces your low-voltage plans will need the following information from you:

1. **The make and model of all equipment running off low-voltage data.** The vendor may request a "cut-sheet book." Cut sheets are data sheets indicating equipment's data connection requirements and size. To make a cut-sheet book, do an internet search for the .PDF cut sheet (also known as the spec sheets) for each piece of equipment. Some cut sheets have multiple models listed, so highlight the model you're using. Once you've gathered all the cut sheets, use a .PDF compiler or merger application to combine the cut sheets into a booklet.

2. **The desired location and height of each piece of equipment running off low-voltage data.** If you're not sure of equipment location or the quantities desired, such as POS equipment, it's often best to earmark multiple low-voltage outlet locations—it's better to have it and not need it! Say you're a barbershop and you're not sure where to put the POS stations. Consider adding low-voltage outlets to both ends of the sales counter. This gives you the ability to move your POS station if, after opening, you determine its current location doesn't make operational sense. It also allows for future expansion of equipment if you need additional POS stations.

3. **The "home-run" location.** This is the distribution spot that all low-voltage cables originate from. It needs to be near your internet modem (since internet gives life to your entire low-voltage system). The "home-run" spot is typically an office, closet, back-of-house shelf, or IT room.

With this information, an architect or low-voltage cabling company should be able to produce a low-voltage plan, along with technical details such as the type of conduit material, cable wire type, end connections, and other plan details that the vendor will specify.

**Self-Installing Low Voltage**

Electrical work can electrocute installers or cause fires if not done properly. Because of this, there's a plethora of code requirements for material use and install procedures.

Electrical work must be performed by a licensed electrician. Low voltage doesn't have enough electrical current to electrocute; therefore, in most cities you can install low-voltage data lines without a license. Installation is fairly straightforward. The tools needed are minimal and cheap. If you're looking to save a buck, consider installing your low-voltage data cables yourself. The process largely involves running conduit (pipe) and pulling wire (data cable) through the conduit. The tricky part is cutting the cable ends with a crimping tool and properly affixing the end pieces (which equipment cords plug into). There are a few additional tasks, such as connecting your low-voltage system to the internet, purchasing a patch panel, and labeling all the wires, but for the most part, the process is straightforward. Tons of DIY literature and video tutorials are available online with further details on required equipment and install specifics.

You can save up to 50 percent by installing low-voltage cables yourself versus hiring a low-voltage cabling company. Consider self-installation only if you have the time and the patience to learn a new skill. I've found that many owners looking to take on additional construction tasks during the planning stage of their project look back and wish they had contracted the work out, not realizing how busy they'd be when installation was needed.

How often do you start a "simple" project that ends up taking three times as long as you planned? That's usually how opening a business goes. There will be a host of projects to keep you busy once construction starts: working with equipment and services vendors, designers, architects, contractors, and marketers; creating operations manuals; accounting; employee hiring; training—you name it. Most people discount the effort needed to open a business.

Remember, an effective owner is an effective delegator. Play to your strengths. Taking on too much will handicap your ability to grow your business.

Note: A lot of equipment requiring low-voltage data also requires electrical work. However you choose to handle low-voltage installation, make sure your architect has a copy of your low-voltage plans and the cut-sheet booklet so that they can correctly draw in any complementing electrical outlets.

**Security System**

Every business should consider getting a security system. There's a ton of options and price points for different security systems, so do your due diligence to find the best setup for your needs. One option is active monitoring. Active monitoring companies are typically cheaper on the front end but more expensive over the lifetime of the system. Account setup and equipment installation cost can range from zero to $1,000. After the initial installation costs, you'll pay a monthly monitoring fee, which can vary from $30 to $150, depending on the security company and equipment options. Installation by a certified technician is often included in the initial proposal, but if you're on a tight budget or like doing things yourself, ask if you can install the system yourself. Installation of some security systems is straightforward, but first see what tools are needed to self-install. At a minimum you'll need a ladder and some spare time!

Primary security features include the following:
1. Motion sensors
2. Door sensors
3. Glass-break sensors
4. Cameras
5. Panic buttons (common in jewelry stores, banks, and some convenience stores)

Determine the level of security coverage your business requires. You can go basic with just a few cameras and door sensors or go all out. Fair warning: Salespeople often propose a system fit for a jewelry store, no matter your concept. At a bare minimum, consider security cameras over cash registers, business access doors, and the office (or wherever valuables such as money, and IT gear are kept). Door sensors for business access doors are also a good idea.

If you don't want to pay a monthly security monitoring fee, then consider buying an off-the shelf system. You can hire your GC or an IT firm to install it, or do it yourself. The cost for these systems is often higher up front but cheaper in the long run, given that there's no active monitoring cost. I've found the big retailers to have some of the most affordable and advanced equipment: Amazon, Best Buy, and Costco, to name a few.

Be wary of contracts! Some vendors require three- to five-year contracts with costly early cancellation fees. Many vendors don't require any contract period, so make sure you read the fine print. The way I see it, if a vendor has a good product, they shouldn't have to lock you into a contract to retain your business.

Get a security system with an app where you can monitor the business from your phone. This has quickly become a standard feature, costing little to no additional money.

You can design your security system at any point of your store's development, but be mindful of any electrical requirements. Most security system cameras and sensors work off low-voltage data, but electricity is typically required for the central control box, which is usually in the office or back-of-house.

**Audio System**

If you'd like the ability to play background music in your store, you'll need an audio system. The process is similar to setting up your security system. Some companies provide the equipment and perform the installation, or you can buy your own equipment and self-install.

If you hire a company to provide and install the equipment, they'll often try to get you locked into a subscription to their music-listening service or a partner's service. Here again, be wary of locking into a long-term service agreement that can be costly to back out of.

Audio systems require electrical for the main control box. Unlike security systems, many speakers require both low-voltage wiring and electricity, although with advancements in audio technology, more and more speakers run off only low voltage and/or a Wi-Fi connection.

Since most owners don't have their security or audio system solidified in the narrow time frame between completion of their floor plan and completion of their electrical drawings, I recommend adding 2 to 4 quadruplex outlets (8 to 16 total plug-in ports) in your office or IT location. This adds electrical outlets for your audio and security systems, along with anything else requiring electricity (computer chargers, Wi-Fi routers, printers, phone equipment, cable modems, a backup power supply system... the list goes on).

There are plenty of audio systems that you can purchase online or in store and then install yourself or via your GC or an IT firm.

Like security system salespeople, audio salespeople often recommend expensive equipment and heavy speaker coverage. Two or three wall-mounted speakers can often cover a 500–1,000-square-foot room. A single cylindrical pendant-mounted speaker (hung from the ceiling) provides excellent 360-degree coverage for small rooms. In most retail concepts, background music is kept to a minimum; therefore it can be difficult to tell the difference in sound quality between standard and high-end speakers. Upgrading to top-of-the-line speakers may not be worth it.

The audio salesperson may advise adding speakers and separate listening controls to the kitchen or break room to keep your staff happy. Although you could do that, there are cheaper alternatives: A boom box or $50 portable speaker serves the same purpose at a fraction of the cost.

To drive home the recurring theme—deciding whether to pay a vendor to install your audio system or self-install— ask yourself if you have the time. Could that time be put to better use? I often see clients tripping over dollars to pick up nickels. They'll delay their project a week to "save" a few hundred bucks on self-installation. How many thousands of dollars in dark rent were forfeited for that install savings? What area of your business was neglected while you were weeds deep in the minutiae?

If Ford Motor Company's production line needs a new IT system, should the CEO install the system himself? HELL, NO! His time is best spent growing the business by making the big decisions, streamlining operations, and forming relationships. Align your priorities! I'm not saying there aren't successful business owners who take on construction and service installation tasks that could be outsourced, but they are often outliers who have a lot of time on their hands.

# PART 4: PERMITTING

**Permit Submittal**

First, figure out whether your project needs to be permitted. Generally speaking, projects that require alterations or additions to wall placements, sprinkler systems, or any mechanical, electrical or plumbing reconfigurations typically require a building permit before doing construction. If your project is a "lipstick" job—requiring only cosmetic alterations such as changes to finishes and painting—you should be able to do the work unpermitted. Work with your local building department to confirm. Some building department websites provide a list of construction activities that don't require a building permit.

Assuming your project needs to be permitted, the first step is defining who's handling the process. Look through your architect's contract. It should show "permit submittal" or "file for permits" as an inclusion or exclusion. If the architect is not handling this, you have some options, listed below. *All applicable plans and permit applications should be submitted to the city immediately after your architect and engineers have completed the plans.*

1.  **Handle it yourself**—It can be a laborious and obfuscating process. You'll need to know what

departments require submittals. For retail concepts, it's often the local fire marshal's office and local building department. Food-service establishments also require submittal to the local health department. In addition to plan submittals at the local level, some states require submittal for items such as wastewater or fire marshal review.

The building department should be the first stop. Call them, or better yet, go and meet with a building department official. Tell them what you're planning to build. They'll be able to advise on the applications and documents required, the submittal format (electronic or in person), whether plans must be approved by one agency before submitting to another agency, and what entities other than the building department require plan submittal. Bring a notebook and take detailed notes. Missing one application or failing to submit plans to a single agency can prolong acquiring building permits for weeks or months. Ask the building department official if there are other jurisdictions that you need to independently submit to or if they will route the paperwork to other agencies on your behalf.

An application for a single department can be 30 pages or more, with questions that may be confusing for a first-timer. Even if they're not contracted to handle plan submittal, architects or consultants will often provide limited assistance. A few cities even have officials who will assist in filling out paperwork.

Many cities still require hard copies of plans and applications that must be physically walked into the building, fire, and health departments. Sometimes the building department will allow for online submittal, whereas another agency requires hand-delivered plans, or vice versa. Some cities paperwork processes are fully online. Find out how your jurisdictions function.

When you handle plan submittal yourself, the plan reviewers may send comments and questions to you. Most of these plan comments are technical in nature and should be forwarded to your architect for answering.

2. **Architect**—Consider having the architect include plan submittal under their scope of work. This is a great option, because architects (even out-of-towners) are generally familiar with the plan submittal form questions and often expedient in getting all forms and plans submitted.
3. **Permit handler**—Hire a permit handler, also called a permit expediter, although I caution against the latter terminology, since many permit handlers can't magically speed up the process. In some big cities where the plan submittal process is convoluted, permit handlers know which

departments need which applications, what needs to be hand-delivered versus emailed, and special sequences of submittals. They also likely already have relationships with specific plan reviewers.

4. **Consultant**—Have your consultant include this under their scope of work, assuming you bring one on to assist with or manage your project. The benefit to using a consultant is that they're already familiar with your project, and they can often line up contractors or vendors to get a jump on their work when the issuance of permits appears imminent.

5. **General contractor**—If you're among the minority of owners who already know what GC you're using, the contractor may be willing to handle permit submittal.

   Since first time retail owners typically go out to bid with multiple contractors, and since the bidding process happens concurrent to plan submittal, I recommend that you *not* allow any of the bidding GC's to handle plan submittal. This muddies the water, and you may find yourself in a sticky situation if the GC that assisted with your plan submittal is not awarding the project. If this is your first time building a store or you're going out to bid with multiple contractors, use one of the first four options.

Before hiring a company to handle plan submittal, see how complicated the process is. The level of complexity varies drastically by city. The plan-submittal process in large cities is generally more complicated than it is in smaller cities or jurisdictions.

It's also worth mentioning that although we talk about the building department as if it's one of three entities (along with fire and health), the building department often comprises 5 to 10 different agencies (such as water, wastewater, mechanical, and so on). Sometimes these department entities have their own specific submittal requirements.

If you decide to outsource plan submittal, understand that any submittal person you hire will fill out the majority of the forms and applications, but you may be required to fill in owner-specific information such as your name, address, legal entity name, or specific vendor information.

The plan-submittal process can be confusing, with different jurisdictions requiring different paperwork. Double-check that you have submitted the required paperwork to all necessary jurisdictions, whether you're doing it yourself or having someone do it for you. Nothing's worse than having your project delayed weeks or months because of one missing form or one missed department. It happens more than you'd think, even when you've entrusted your project to a professional outside handler.

Find out whether your city has a fast-track, or expedited, plan review process. It's often a pay-to-play system with varying costs. Not all cities offer expedited plan review, nor do all project types meet the requirements for expedited review. If yours does qualify, consider paying the extra cost. Time is money, and there's generally greater upside to fast-tracking the opening of your business. Besides, the clock's ticking toward the countdown to rent commencement!

When submitting your plans and applications, ask when you can expect the first round of comments from plan reviewers. Track that date, and follow up with the city if you haven't heard from them by then. Crazy stuff happens, and cities do lose permit applications from time to time. Sorry, but receiving building permits without any requests for revisions to your plans that then need to be resubmitted to the city is akin to winning the lottery. Two to three rounds of city plan review comments is common.

Once plans have been submitted to the city, request the online permit number. With this number you can go online and track the status of your building permit. Although many cities have an online permit portal for tracking the status of permits, some cities are old-school, requiring you to call or email them for updates.

I always call the different departments that require plan submittal to see how long they're averaging to review and approve plans. Take their estimates with a grain of salt, because it's *impossible* to truly know how long it will take to acquire building permits. Estimates are generally rosy and based on one set of plan review comments. But what if you go through two or three rounds of comments? Or what if one of the two mechanical reviewers quits the job or goes on vacation, doubling the mechanical review time? What if the city just got a big influx of applications for building permits right before you submitted? Since a building permit won't be issued until all agencies have signed off on the plans, the last agency to sign off (taking the longest) will determine how long it takes to receive permits. Regardless of the many variables, it's nice to call the city and inquire about timing so you know if you're looking at six to eight weeks or six to eight months.

## Picking Up Building Permits

When the building permit is issued, you'll likely need to physically pick it up. Ask what's needed to release or pick up the permit. There's often a release fee, and costs vary dramatically—from a few hundred to tens of thousands of dollars. Most cities require your contractor to pick up the building permit. If that's the case, you'll need to provide payment to your GC, because GCs exclude building permit fees from their construction bids (because of fluctuating permit costs).

Trying to budget for your project but not sure whether the building permit will cost $500 or $15,000? Call the city and ask. Start with the building department. The building department is usually good at outlining the process for other jurisdictions. Sometimes there's a flat fee, but it's often a sliding-scale fee based on the value of construction. For the latter, permit fees for a $300,000 build-out would cost approximately three times more than a $100,000 build-out. For example, I recently did a project where the city had the following permit cost structure:

$6.50 per $1,000 of the contracted construction cost for the building department review fee

+

$3.25 per $1,000 of the contracted construction cost for the health department review fee

+

A set $350 fee for the fire marshal office review

The construction cost was $320,000. In total, building permit fees were $3,470 ($2,080 for building, $1,040 for health, and $350 for fire).

**Physical Plans**

Even in the digital age, probably half of all cities have at least one agency that requires that physical plans and applications be sent in for review. Why? Some cities and states are just behind the times with regulations that have not kept up with technology. In other circumstances, it's believed that wet stamping (done by a physical ink pad, not computer generated), along with handwritten signatures, is a sign of authenticity that a registered architect or engineer produced the plans. Regardless, when a city requires physical plans, it means someone must hand-deliver them. You usually cannot mail them in.

If you're using an out-of-town architect or consultant, you'll be that courier. Unless you win the lottery, there will be city plan review comments requiring multiple trips to and from the city offices with revised drawings addressing those comments. Even more fun, the different departments are often in different buildings, sometimes across town.

Typically, a city requiring physical plans will need multiple plan sets so that various reviewers can review your project simultaneously. Each set of comments can trigger the need for additional plans for all the plan reviewers. A full-size set of plans (24 by 36 inches) can cost more than $100 to print. There's also the expedited shipping cost for out-of-town architects to ship plans to you. Depending on how many sets of plans a city requires, shipping and printing costs can range from a few hundred dollars to a couple thousand dollars.

Remember, approximately half of all cities accept digital plans, meaning no shipping and printing costs. Because of this, many architects exclude printing and shipping fees from their base cost and then bill the client based on actual cost. If this is the case, make sure you allocate additional monies in your budget for plan-printing fees if your city requires physical copies. Smaller jurisdictions typically require fewer sets of plans and fewer rounds of comments. Consider budgeting $500 when building in small cities and $1,000 for larger cities.

# PART 5: PRECONSTRUCTION

**What's a General Contractor?**

A general contractor orchestrates and manages all construction activities. They oversee job-site safety, coordination of subcontractors, city inspections, and payment to subcontractors. A general contractor allows for business owners to bid their project to a single entity (the GC), at which point the GC will solicit bids from various subcontractors to wrap into an all-encompassing project bid. A GC specializing in tenant improvement construction will have three key players with whom you'll work: an estimator, a project manager, and a superintendent.

1. The **estimator** is the first general contractor team member you'll typically engage with (besides the firm's owner, or possibly a lead generator). The estimator's duties entail soliciting bids from subcontractors and reviewing the plans to ensure that all needed subcontractors have provided costs for the various components of construction. The estimator will wrap subcontractors' bids into an all-encompassing project bid. The estimator is typically your point of contact for bid review and cost negotiations.

2.  The **project manager** (PM) does just what the term suggests: manages the project. The PM oversees multiple projects for a general contractor. The project manager is typically your point person for communication and project dialog. In some companies, the project manager and estimator are one and the same. The PM will appoint a superintendent to manage daily job-site activities. In a company's hierarchy, the PM is generally above the superintendent, although it's not uncommon to work with a contractor where the superintendent is the first point of contact and the PM plays an oversight and administrative role. So as not to step on anyone's toes, ask the PM who communication should be run through.

3.  The **superintendent** is the boots-on-the-ground person, overseeing daily job-site activities. They are the first person to arrive at the job site and the last one to leave. They manage job-site safety and security and inspections, and oversee subcontractors' work. It depends on a project's nature and size, but most TI projects valued above $75,000 warrant a full-time on-site superintendent.

4.  Because of the small size of many general contractors, especially those who specialize in retail TI work, it's not uncommon to work directly with the firm's owners, who may wear the hat of estimator and project manager, although the owner should *always* have a dedicated superintendent for each project.

**Early GC Engagement**

If you've never used a contractor and you're looking for the best construction price, be careful not to engage with a sole GC too early, especially if they approached you. Why? A contractor who knows they're the sole bidder tends to bid the project higher than when they're competing against other contractors. Also, construction costs often come in higher than initially estimated. When this happens and there's only one bid, it's only natural to wonder if another GC can do the project for less. Then you go back out to bid, delaying the time to acquire a contractor by two to four weeks.

**Ethics of Bidding**

When bidding the project, there are a few ethical components to adhere to. First, bid the project to multiple contractors only if you're fully open to using any of them. Having a GC you already know you'll be using but soliciting additional bids for cost reference is wrong. A good contractor spends many hours reviewing plans, acquiring and compiling subcontractors' costs, and visiting the job site to familiarize themselves with existing conditions. They do this free of charge with the understanding that they have a fair chance of getting the project.

Don't share bid numbers. When a GC asks how his numbers stack up against other bidders, know the difference between speaking in cost generalities and explicitly providing another contractor's number. Not only is this unethical, but it's becoming illegal in more and more jurisdictions. Although prosecution of bid-rigging mostly focuses on multimillion- and billion-dollar projects, the Sherman Act prohibits bid-rigging by anticompetitive methods such as providing a competitor's cost. Some states and localities have adopted additional laws to further ensure a fair and competitive bid process.

Let's say you've received a $305,000 bid and a $340,000 bid. The high bidder asks how his bid stacks up against the competition and wants to know what he can do to win the project. An acceptable answer would be "To get the project, you'll need to come down significantly." An unacceptable answer would be "You'll need to come in under the other contractor's current bid of $305,000." I usually say something along the lines of, "All the bids came in really close. Any cost reductions you can produce will help your efforts in winning the project."

Ironically, if you provide a contractor with other GCs' bid numbers, *you're likely hurting yourself*. How? Since there's little wiggle room in a contractor's bid, the GC may undercut their competition to get the project, at which point they're likely in the red (currently taking a loss on the project). To get back to profitability, they'll squeeze it out of their subs, use inferior materials, or hit you with change orders. Dealing with a bunch of change orders makes a project miserable—they're frustrating, can lead to project delays, and are, of course, costly.

It's fine to negotiate, but don't overdo it. If multiple contractors have close numbers, tell them to go sharpen their pencils. Ask for a revised "best and final" number. Then make your decision based on the contractors' second round of prices if possible. Letting one GC have an additional round or two of cost revisions isn't fair to the other contractors. Further, it unnecessarily prolongs the bidding process, and any additional price revisions will be minor in amount, likely not justifying any project delays incurred.

After you've awarded the project to a contractor, reach out to the other bidder(s) to let them know you're going with another contractor but that you appreciate their time bidding the project. It's never fun being the bearer of bad news. Because of this, it's human nature to put off or altogether avoid giving the news to the contractors who didn't get the project. The right thing to do is let the other bidders know soon after you've made your decision. You'd be surprised with how well received a prompt and polite "rejection" notice is. Just remember, many GCs lose more projects than they get. It's just part of business. They'll appreciate finding out promptly so they can shift their resources to the next project. My most common reply is something along the lines of, "I appreciate you letting me know. Please keep us in mind for your next store. We'd love to bid the next one." Seriously! I prefer a phone call (more personable), but emails work fine.

**Finding the Right General Contractor**

Most owners pick a contractor based on cost. As such, for the typical tenant improvement build-out valued between $75,000 and $1,000,000, the most cost-effective general contractors are often smaller in nature—typically, firms that do $5 million to $50 million a year in work.

Find a contractor whose area of expertise matches your concept. A GC who primarily does construction other than tenant improvement work such as residential construction is not advised. Food service is a different beast altogether. If your business is a restaurant or bar, find a GC with recent experience in such.

Are you in a franchise organization? Using a GC who has built a previous one of your franchise partners' concepts is generally recommended, given the GC's familiarity with your store. The second one is always easier and faster!

Creating the right-size GC bid pool is important. It can also be fickle. If the project is bid to too many contractors, the bidders will likely find out and drop out of your bid pool because their chances of getting the job are low. Or the GCs provide a high, haphazardly put-together bid for you. Alternatively, if the project is bid to only one or two contractors, and a GC drops out of the bid pool (a common occurrence in hot construction markets), having a single bid limits your options and leaves you wondering whether you've secured a competitive price. The ideal bid pool is three GCs, four maximum (assuming you don't have prior experience using a contractor). To hedge your bets against the chances of contractors declining a project, call them while plans are being drawn up to see if they believe they'll have the time and manpower to take on the job around the time you believe building permits will be ready.

GCs are a dime a dozen: They're everywhere. Below are recommended avenues for finding GCs (in no particular order).
1. Ask your architect.
2. Do an internet search.
3. Get references from your real estate broker.
4. Ask family or friends who have built similar businesses.
5. Ask neighboring retail tenants.
6. Ask your landlord. In particular, find out who built the "shell" of your retail center. This can be a valuable GC, because the shell builder will know of

any nuances in your space. I especially like using the shell GC if they're actively building the retail center. Why? The shell GC can often get a head start on construction. They'll also use the same shell subcontractor, which helps mitigate issues and guesswork for tying into existing building infrastructure.

**Required Subcontractors**

A general contractor will use his preferred subcontractors when possible, but there are usually a few subcontractors that your landlord will require you to use. Look through your lease, or ask your landlord's representative for the name and contact information of required subs. Typical landlord-required subs are listed below.

1.  **Roofing subcontractor**—The most common landlord-required subcontractor is their roofer. If you're making plumbing alterations, adding a kitchen hood, or making HVAC mechanical additions to your business, a roofer will be required to cut and patch rooftop holes to accommodate those systems.

2.  **Fire sprinkler subcontractor**– If your space is sprinklered, the landlord has likely run the system into your unit, with sprinkler heads in an upright fixed position throughout the space. These sprinkler lines will need to be "turned down" in areas where you're adding overhead coverage, i.e., ceilings and ductwork.

3.  **Fire alarm subcontractor**—If your space is sprinklered, odds are good it has a fire alarm. To assure continuity of your system and the shopping center's system, using the

subcontractor who installed the shopping center's fire alarm is sometimes required.

**Bidding the Project**

Once plans are complete, the architect will email you electronic plan copies. Concurrent to submitting the plans to the city for building permits, the plans should be sent electronically to bidding contractors, along with any supplemental support documents that you or your architect see necessary such as owner-provided millwork drawings or interior-design plans. In the email to bidding GCs, include contact information for any landlord-required subcontractors. Next, provide a deadline for receiving completed bids. Two weeks is industry standard in normal construction markets. If your space is being built in a "hot" market, GCs may need three to four weeks to produce a bid, because it can take longer for them to receive bids from all their subcontractors. *The best way to get bids on time is to send a reminder note to bidders one week before bids are due.*

Once bids are received, it's time to review them and decide who to call back to further discuss their numbers. Assuming the contractors' bids correctly reflect the scope of work needed, there will not be a lot of wiggle room between an initial bid and the price you'll contract at. If the GC is hungry for your business and you're a hard bargainer, a *best-case* downward price revision will be 5–15 percent. Why so little? Because the GC's bid is made up of maybe 10–20 subcontractors' numbers, which typically represent 76–92 percent of the overall construction cost. The remaining 8–24 percent [13] are costs the general contractor directly controls, known as "general conditions" (mainly superintendent and project management personnel costs) and their overhead and profit (OH&P). A hungry general contractor may be willing to cut his cost, but most subcontractors stick at or near their original number.

If you've hired the architect or a consultant to assist with construction management, make sure they're involved with bid review. Rely on their expertise, because bid review can be technical in nature, and having a seasoned adviser assist with it can really pay off.

Since we know an initial bid won't change much, set your sights on the lowest bidder, pushing the others aside. If the second contractor has pricing within 5–10 percent of the low bidder, you may want to work with both the first and second bidder. Whomever you call back, don't just request a "best and final" bid. It's important to carefully review the scope of work and clarify any inaccuracies found, as well as discuss project expectations.

There are times when you don't need to negotiate pricing. You'd never haggle over the price of your groceries, but it doesn't hurt to request lower costs on spend-y proposals. The more expensive the proposal, the larger the potential cost savings from negotiating costs. Asking for lower pricing takes a few seconds, and the worst a vendor can do is say no. I always request lower pricing from a contractor's initial bid proposal. You should too.

**Contractor Vetting**

If you've never worked with a contractor before, they should be properly vetted before you contract with them. By using a contractor, you're entrusting an important and costly project to their safekeeping. You may also be required to pay the contractor a deposit to the tune of tens or hundreds of thousands of dollars before any work commences. Request references from previous work done, and then ask those references the following questions:

1. Was the GC easy to work with?
2. Did the GC perform per expectations?
3. Was the GC reasonable with change orders or did you feel nickel and dimed?
4. Did the GC keep to the construction timeline?
5. Were you pleased with the final product?

Confirm that the GC's licenses and insurance are current. Most lenders, city officials, and landlords require this information, so get copies of the contractor's license and insurance when requesting a contract. Some general contractors' licenses cover their subcontractors. If they don't, it's worth verifying that their subcontractors are current on their paperwork as well.

If you want to be thorough, ask the GC for his mechanical, electrical, and plumbing (MEP) subcontractors' information, then ask those subs for references and vet them. These subs typically do the lion's share of the construction work. Using inadequate MEP subcontractors can be costly, lead to project delays, and drive an owner crazy.

When bidding a project, take note of how the bidders conduct themselves. Funny thing: I find a correlation between a contractor's ability to bid a project on time and their ability to meet build-out timelines, even when the estimator and project manager are different people in the company. Why? Because a company's work culture is systemic. Working with a responsive estimator who's able to hit deadlines is indicative of a project manager and superintendent who will follow suit.

If a contractor can't produce a bid on time, how do you expect them to properly manage the build-out? When they claim the bid was late because subcontractors were slow to provide numbers, that leads to arguably greater worry about their ability to perform per expectations. Those subs were late to provide numbers, presumably because they have a lot of work on their plate. So now you're trusting that they'll be able to make it to your job site when needed? It sure doesn't inspire confidence.

Did the contractor and his subs visit the job site to verify existing conditions *during* the bidding process? Or did they base their costs on assumed site attributes? If they did the latter, they'll do everything possible to stick you with the cost of any wrongly assumed site attributes when they start building.

I love getting requests for information (RFIs) and questions during the bid process. To me it shows that a contractor and his subs have actually reviewed the plans and are making an honest effort to flush out any project ambiguities now, rather than during construction.

## Construction Costs and Change Orders

You've selected your GC and signed their contract for, say, $250,000. You've set aside $250,000 for construction and not a penny more. On to the next item, right? Wrong! A tough part of building anything is understanding that the dollar amount you initially agreed to is rarely the final amount you'll pay. Why? Because of change orders.

A change order is a request from contractors for additional monies. Although there may be construction mistakes requiring subcontractors to rectify problems out of pocket, most projects also have road bumps come up that require owner money to fix. There's a whole host of reasons for change orders: unforeseen job-site conditions, city inspectors requesting changes, design change requests from owners or contractors, utility company issues, a lapse in the responsibility matrix, or issues with the plans.

Quite truthfully, errors, missing items, or ambiguity among construction documents accounts for a sizable chunk of change orders. I'm not one for excuses, but I'll often give the design professionals a break. They're tasked with producing plans encompassing thousands of design elements, with sometimes the difference between a singular and plural word resulting in a change order. Humans are the ones creating these plans. Mistakes happen. Some GCs and their subs are better at covering the costs of minor plan discrepancies than others. A good contractor once told me, "There's no perfect set of plans." Even as someone who delves into plan drafting and is a bit of a perfectionist, I'd have to agree. There's always something missing or incorrect.

Some change orders result from an architect forgetting to include certain items in a set of plans, but bear in mind that had the architect included them from the get-go, initial construction costs would have been that much higher. For instance, if the architect forgot to add wainscot to 25 percent of the walls, the GC's wainscot subcontractor would have provided the cost to wainscot only the walls shown. Had the architect drawn wainscot on

100 percent of the walls, the initial wainscot cost would have been 25 percent higher. It's maddening to see project costs go up, but if it's any consolation, your construction costs would have been just as high if everything had been initially included in the plans.

**Mitigating Change-Order Costs**

There are things you can do to mitigate the extent and cost of change orders. For starters, you can hire a consultant or architect to perform a secondary plan review. I often spend a few hours doing a deep-dive review of all construction documents. I've yet to find fewer than a half dozen errors or omissions on a set of plans.

Next, review the GC's "exclusions" page of their construction bid. The exclusions outline any items the GC assumes will be handled by the owner, owner's vendor, or landlord, or that he simply believes is not needed for the project. Contractors do not allocate any monies to items they've excluded from the project. From time to time you'll run into a dishonest GC who excludes items that are clearly part of the required scope of work in order to be the low bidder and get the job. Don't fall prey to this; *review all exclusions carefully!*

One of the most important items involves bid review. Spend the time to review the GC's costs line by line to see what numbers appear off or missing. Don't be afraid to question potential bid discrepancies. And yes, you should discuss potentially missing items.

Nothing in life's free, and certainly not in construction. If you know the plans call for GC-provided millwork, but it doesn't appear to be in the GC's bid, odds are the GC forgot to get millwork costs or he assumed it would be owner provided. Not saying anything, then "trapping" the GC into providing the millwork after signing their contract "because it's shown on the drawings" probably won't get you anywhere—at least not for expensive items such as a high-dollar millwork package. Not saying anything will only prolong your project. When the discrepancy is discovered, the millwork installation will be delayed for many weeks as you or the GC scramble to find vendors, get millwork quotes, and attempt to expedite the production and installation of the millwork package.

As painful as it is, discussing potential missing items during bid review will avoid disputes and hasten the completion of your project. It may even save you money. How? Once you've locked into a contract with a GC, he and his subs don't always provide competitive pricing. They know you're not likely to go through the headaches and paperwork of finding another GC to perform the additional work. Without a viable alternative, even a legitimate change order becomes an opportune moment for the GC or subcontractor to jack up the cost. Feel like you're being hustled on price? Consult with your consultant or architect, or get a comparative bid from another contractor.

Getting back to that $250,000 initial construction bid. First and foremost, *don't get wed to the initial contract amount.* A small proportion of retail projects, possibly 10 percent, get through construction without cost overruns. Unfortunately, most projects have issues come up that require additional owner-provided money to redress.

Because of this, it's prudent to carry an additional 10–15 percent of monies above and beyond the initial construction contract amount for change orders and unforeseen anomalies. Some projects have overruns in excess of 15 percent, but the majority stay at or under 15 percent. If you're unable to provide contingency funds above the initial contract amount, please take a moment to consider whether continuing forward with the development of your business is a good idea. Walking away from a business that's 90 percent built out is devastating.

**Contract Allowances**

In the contractor's bid or contract documents, you may see costs listed as allowances (or sometimes "budgets"). An allowance is a nonbinding estimate that's subject to change. A GC's contract should always say whether the allowance covers the materials, installation, or both. Here are some common reasons for allowances:

1. The GC was unable to get a subcontractor's cost by the bid due date.
2. The owner has not yet selected certain design elements or finishes.
3. The plans were unclear on the exact scope of work.
4. The scope of work is approximate and not fully known.

Let's assume the GC is expected to furnish and install flooring. You're eager to start construction but don't want to wait another week for the GC to solidify flooring costs, so you execute the GC's contract, knowing a $15,000 flooring allowance is included in the bid. A week later, the

GC receives a subcontractor's bid. With the GC's markups, the cost is $18,500. At this point, the GC would issue a change order for the $3,500 difference.

If you're not happy that the cost came in higher than the contractor estimated, it's okay to ask the contractor to seek additional bids. I've even had clients take on the duty of soliciting additional bids on the contractor's behalf.

Conversely, if the cost comes in under the allowance amount, the GC will owe you a credit.

If the contractor claims the cost came in at the same amount as his allowance, there's no harm in requesting a copy of the subcontractor's bid amount to confirm it, since that's quite a coincidence and may indicate that the cost came in under the GC's estimate but the contractor is pocketing the savings—which should be your money.

A contractor always remembers to request additional money when actual costs come in above the allowance amount, but at times "forgets" to credit owners when actual costs come in under the allowance amount, since many owners fail to follow up on the matter.

It's generally accepted that GCs can include their overhead and profit (OH&P) markups in allowances so long as the markup is in line with their base bid's overall OH&P percentage. All things being equal, a GC should also credit any of their OH&P markups on allowances when costs come in under the allowance estimate.

Allowances require extra paperwork and time for both contractors and owners, so avoid them when possible.

**Awarding the Project**

You've reviewed the contractor's bid, reviewed the scope of work, and discussed any exclusions and allowances. All looks good and you're ready to award the project. It's time to let the GC know you're okay with their bid and request a contract. When requesting a contract, ask it to be in American Institute of Architects (AIA) format. AIA format is the industry standard for contract documents. It's considered fair to both parties, even preferential to architects and business owners. An AIA document communicates payment draw schedules, dispute handling, workmanship requirements, and a whole lot more. For the last 50 years, AIA documents have been revised every decade, with the 2017 version being the latest and greatest. Presumably in 2027 a new version will come out. Make sure you're working off the latest version.

Once the GC provides a contract, it's advisable to have a construction contract attorney review it on your behalf. Even though AIA documents are industry standard, there are different types of agreements based on project type, and contractors often strip down or delete sections—not necessarily out of malevolence, but often because they believe a certain section is irrelevant to your project. There may also be blank sections of the contract that they fill in with nonindustry-standard verbiage or payment terms.

**Liquidated Damages**

I've got some bad news about the project completion time listed on your GC's contract. Unless you've specifically requested a liquidated damages clause, the quoted build time means nothing. Why is this noteworthy? The majority of construction projects are delayed. The best way to get your GC to complete the project per the schedule or be compensated for contractor-related construction delays is to request a liquidated damages clause in the construction contract. This document says that if the GC fails to substantially complete the project by a described date, the GC must pay the client daily penalties, typically $250 to $1,500 per *calendar* day that the GC is late to reach substantial completion.

Note: Liquidated damages contracts often base penalties on *calendar* days (all seven days in a week), not business days (Monday–Friday).

Before you go rushing to see what AIA section to include in your GC's contract (it's AIA A101 2017, Section 4.5), first consider the following: Few first-time business owners realize the probability of project delays. Of those who do, even fewer do anything about it, i.e., have their contractor agree to a liquidated damages clause. As such, many small-time contractors are not accustomed to seeing liquidated damages clauses. Even GCs who are familiar with them may not agree to a contract with a liquidated damages clause. Why? There's an argument that many aspects of construction are outside of a general contractor's direct control—subcontractors' schedules, inspectors' schedules, weather, owners' vendors, unforeseen conditions, and landlord restrictions. Some GCs don't want to be on the hook for other people's performances or lack thereof. On the flip side, you're paying the contractor good money to be the master orchestrator of your project. A determined bull will always clear its own path.

I've had contractors refuse to enter into a contract with a liquidated damages clause unless there's also a performance bonus, meaning they receive daily bonuses (typically equal to the damages amount) for each day they finish ahead of schedule. Personally, I find it fair. If a contractor is on the hook for any delays, they should also be rewarded for completing the project ahead of schedule. The odds of paying out bonuses are slim, because projects tend to lengthen, *not* shorten. The name of the game is getting your store open as quickly as possible to start making money, so if the GC finishes early, paying a bonus should be welcomed.

*Before* discussing liquidated damages or bonuses, have the contractor provide a quoted build time. If they already know you want a liquidated damages clause, they'll likely add extra time to their build-out schedule to assure they don't have to pay out any damages, thus increasing the chance of you paying unnecessary bonuses.

If you choose to pursue a liquidated damages clause in the contract, make darn sure you're not holding up the project, because the GC will add up all the owner-delayed time and offset it against the agreed-upon build period. Far too often, owners are their own worst enemies, causing many delays. When this happens, it can be a back-and-forth of who's more at fault. Does the GC owe you money for liquidated damages, or do you owe the GC money for owner delays and the additional time the GC had to spend on the project because of them? The long and short of it: Run a tight ship. Be available throughout construction to answer questions and address issues. Act expeditiously when the contractor is reliant on you for answers. If this is not possible, consider bringing on a consultant to be your advocate.

Here are some common reasons for owner delays:

1. Failing to get owner-provided equipment to the job site when needed
2. Making design changes
3. Not addressing contractor RFIs in a timely manner
4. Not addressing contractor change orders or issues in a timely manner
5. Failure to make material selections in a timely manner
6. Failure to set up utility services on time
7. Failure to make draw payments to the contractor on time

**Landlord Turnover**

The turnover-to-tenant date (or possession date) starts the countdown to rent commencement (assuming there's a free-rent period), common-area maintenance (CAM) expenses, and utilities fees. Although you want to accept the space to start construction, there are times when you should refuse possession of the space. Why is this? And how can you refuse possession?

Let's start with the *why*. If a landlord turns over the space but you don't have building permits or a contractor lined up, odds are you're marching toward paying dark rent. If possible, you want to refuse possession until you have a contractor ready and building permits issued.

Now to the *how*. Whether you're going into a new building or a second-generation space, you may have negotiated a landlord work letter in which the landlord is responsible for installing certain site attributes for your store. Usually, it's required that these items be installed before the landlord turns over the space. When the landlord gives you possession of the space, review the work letter (which is in your lease) to confirm that all landlord-provided items have been properly installed.

Let's assume the landlord gives you possession of the space. You've reviewed the lease, and per the work letter, the landlord is expected to build your demising wall (the wall shared with your neighboring tenant) and install patio fencing, but neither of these have been installed. Document the existing condition, then in written correspondence to the landlord, refuse possession of the space until the demising wall and fence have been properly installed in accordance with the work letter.

The lease verbiage may allow the landlord to complete his work during the free-rent period or concurrent with your construction. Even if this is the case, it doesn't hurt to email the landlord in an attempt to refuse possession until all landlord work has been completed. *Landlords will often wait to turn over the space or extend the free-rent period in these circumstances even if they technically don't have to.*

If you're going into a new building that's still under construction, there are likely items above and beyond the work letter that the landlord's contractor must complete to fully finish construction of the center: landscaping, parking lot striping, inspections, and more. If this is the case, in addition to confirming that all work-letter items have been installed, verify that substantial completion of the shell has occurred. Substantial completion of a building means the shell contractor has completed all work and inspections as agreed upon between the landlord and shell contractor, and the building has been turned over to the landlord. At this point, the building should be ready for tenant improvement construction.

It can be hard to determine exactly when a landlord has turned the space over to you. If you haven't received an official notice, the day you receive the keys to your retail space is often considered the turnover-to-tenant date by a landlord. Be careful when accepting keys, and always verify that the landlord has fulfilled their work-letter obligations.

### Insurance

Give it time and something will go wrong. Make sure you're covered with business insurance when that happens. Different businesses require different coverages, so I won't discuss specific coverage needs. Instead, I'll discuss the nuances, timing, and steps needed to acquire insurance.

Once you have a signed lease, send a copy of your lease's insurance requirements to insurance companies for quotes. The underwriter will spend one to two weeks creating a policy that satisfies your landlord's insurance minimums. The insurance provider will likely discuss additional coverages that you may need that are not required by your landlord. Do your homework. The more coverage options you add, the more money the insurance company makes, but additional coverages may well be needed, such as commercial auto coverage if you have a delivery car that you or employees will use.

Insurance rates vary, so consider getting two to three quotes. I've found that bundling your business insurance with your home and auto policy is often cheaper than working with a business insurance company alone.

Some leases require you to be covered within 30 days of lease signing, so be cognizant of when you need to start the process, because sometimes you have to find an insurer immediately after signing a lease. It can take two to four weeks to get insurance, because it takes time to define policy options, wait for the insurer to underwrite the policy, execute the contract, and pay any policy activation fees.

Make sure your insurance provider "staggers" the kick-in of coverages so that you're not paying for, say, workers compensation coverage while you're still working on design or construction. Pre-open insurance can be half the cost of coverage when you're open.

Even if your lease doesn't stipulate early coverage, considering getting covered from the day you sign your lease. Pre-open insurance is relatively inexpensive, and it covers you while design professionals are walking through the job site or construction activities are occurring.

If you're part of a franchise, your franchisor will have insurance requirements. In this case, give policy providers a copy of your landlord's insurance requirements *and* franchise requirements. The insurance provider will create a policy that satisfies both parties' needs. If your landlord requires $1 million in commercial general liability coverage but your franchisor requires $2 million, the policy would cover the greater of the two.

**Builders Risk Insurance**

Builders risk insurance protects against loss of furniture, fixtures, equipment, and construction materials during the construction phase of your project to theft, flood, fire, and certain acts of God. Refer to the insurance policy agreement for specifics, because sometimes there are goofy stipulations, such as clauses in which FF&E or materials stored off-site or further than 50 feet from the work site are not insured. Builders risk is an optional insurance coverage that landlords typically don't require, but I'm a proponent of it. Nearly every year I have at least one client who must make a claim against their builders risk insurance, with the most common issue being theft of materials or FF&E.

Some contractors offer builders risk, but I've found their rates to be higher on average than getting it through your business insurer. For a construction cost valued at $300,000 with $150,000 in FF&E, expect to pay $400–$1,200 during the entirety of construction for builders risk. Like vehicle insurance, the deductible amount varies and will affect your policy rate. If you get builders risk insurance, have the policy in place *before* materials or equipment arrive at the job site.

Builders risk is not a supplement to your general insurance policy; rather it's in addition to your policy, and typically expires upon the completion of construction.

### Construction Payment Structures

There are two common payment structures: "milestone" and "completion-based," with the latter being commonplace for retail and restaurant construction projects valued at more than approximately $100,000.

1. **Milestone-based payments**—A less common payment structure, milestone payments are based on physical construction milestones, often centered on passing inspections or installation of specific materials and equipment. Although this payment structure is tied to a tangible milestone, timing between payments can be sporadic, resulting in either contractors having to front costs or owners making excessive draw payments during certain draw cycles. Below is an example:
   - 10 percent draw payment upon notice to proceed from client
   - 25 percent draw payment upon passing of underground inspections
   - 25 percent draw payment upon passing of rough-in inspections
   - 30 percent draw payment upon completion of overhead inspections and commencement of finish carpentry installation
   - 10 percent draw payment upon

   A) completion of all work indicated in the construction documents;

   B) issuance of a certificate of occupancy; and

   C) receipt of lien waivers from the general contractor, subcontractors, and material suppliers.

2. **Completion-based payments**—Industry standard, completion-based payments entail an initial down

payment, followed by monthly progress payments based on the percentage of work completed.

Work completed is broken out by the collective sum of all subcontractor work. The draw payment amount (typically monthly for projects in excess of 8–12 weeks) is a calculation of the collective work completed by all subcontractors, divided by the total construction amount, minus previous payments made.

As you'll see with the example below, the original construction amount was $467,000. There have been $6,602.25 in change orders thus far, bringing the revised construction amount to $473,602.25. Collectively, the GC claims that 55.01 percent of construction has been completed. The contractor bills the client for $118,374.45. Here's how we get to this number:

> $473,602.25 (current contract sum) times .5501 (work completion amount) = $260,528.60, times .90 (accounting for 10 percent retainage) = $234,475.74 (current completion amount), minus $116,099.82 (previous payments made) = $118,374.45 (total amount due).

| Description | Original Budget | Approved Change Orders | Revised Budget | Previous Completed & Stored | Current Invoice Work Completed | Current Invoice Stored Material | Total Completed & Stored | % Complete | Balance To Finish | Retainage |
|---|---|---|---|---|---|---|---|---|---|---|
| 01 31 00: General Conditions / Project Management | $52,335.00 | $1,127.25 | $53,462.25 | $15,700.50 | $16,827.75 | $.00 | $32,528.25 | 60.84 | $20,934.00 | $3,252.82 |
| 01 71 13: Mobilization | $67,300.00 | $.00 | $67,300.00 | $67,300.00 | $.00 | $.00 | $67,300.00 | 100.00 | $.00 | $6,730.00 |
| 01 74 00: Waste & Incidental Demolition | $7,650.00 | $.00 | $7,650.00 | $3,825.00 | $1,147.50 | $.00 | $4,972.50 | 65.00 | $2,677.50 | $497.25 |
| 03 30 00: Concrete | $4,675.00 | $5,475.00 | $10,150.00 | $4,675.00 | $5,475.00 | $.00 | $10,150.00 | 100.00 | $.00 | $1,015.00 |
| 04 21 13: Masonry Veneer | $15,215.00 | $.00 | $15,215.00 | $.00 | $.00 | $.00 | $.00 | .00 | $15,215.00 | $.00 |
| 05 55 00: Miscellaneous Metals | $5,844.00 | $.00 | $5,844.00 | $.00 | $5,844.00 | $.00 | $5,844.00 | 100.00 | $.00 | $584.40 |
| 06 10 00: Rough & Finish Carpentry | $7,641.00 | $.00 | $7,641.00 | $.00 | $.00 | $.00 | $.00 | .00 | $7,641.00 | $.00 |
| 06 22 00: Millwork / Bar Construction | $11,475.00 | $.00 | $11,475.00 | $.00 | $.00 | $.00 | $.00 | .00 | $11,475.00 | $.00 |
| 07 50 00: Membrane Roofing | $2,550.00 | $.00 | $2,550.00 | $.00 | $.00 | $.00 | $.00 | .00 | $2,550.00 | $.00 |
| 08 10 00: Doors, Frames & Hardware | $9,648.00 | $.00 | $9,648.00 | $.00 | $.00 | $.00 | $.00 | .00 | $9,648.00 | $.00 |
| 08 50 00: Windows / Glass Glazing / Mirrors | $1,989.00 | $.00 | $1,989.00 | $.00 | $.00 | $.00 | $.00 | .00 | $1,989.00 | $.00 |
| 09 21 00: Drywall | $24,353.00 | $.00 | $24,353.00 | $6,088.25 | $6,575.31 | $.00 | $12,663.56 | 52.00 | $11,689.44 | $1,266.35 |
| 09 30 00: Tile | $5,525.00 | $.00 | $5,525.00 | $.00 | $.00 | $.00 | $.00 | .00 | $5,525.00 | $.00 |
| 09 91 00: Painting | $7,038.00 | $.00 | $7,038.00 | $1,759.50 | $.00 | $.00 | $1,759.50 | 25.00 | $5,278.50 | $175.95 |
| 09 97 23: Floor Sealing | $2,794.00 | $.00 | $2,794.00 | $.00 | $.00 | $.00 | $.00 | .00 | $2,794.00 | $.00 |
| 10 44 16: Accessories / Fire Extinguishers / Etc | $7,905.00 | $.00 | $7,905.00 | $.00 | $.00 | $.00 | $.00 | .00 | $7,905.00 | $.00 |
| 21 00 00: Fire Suppression | $9,605.00 | $.00 | $9,605.00 | $1,440.75 | $6,723.50 | $.00 | $8,164.25 | 85.00 | $1,440.75 | $816.43 |
| 22 00 00: Plumbing | $63,750.00 | $.00 | $63,750.00 | $12,750.00 | $28,687.50 | $.00 | $41,437.50 | 65.00 | $22,312.50 | $4,143.75 |
| 23 00 00: Heating, Ventilation & Air Conditioning | $97,750.00 | $.00 | $97,750.00 | $9,775.00 | $48,875.00 | $.00 | $58,650.00 | 60.00 | $39,100.00 | $5,865.00 |
| 23 38 13: Ansul System for Hood | $5,100.00 | $.00 | $5,100.00 | $.00 | $.00 | $.00 | $.00 | .00 | $5,100.00 | $.00 |
| 26 00 00: Electrical | $56,858.00 | $.00 | $56,858.00 | $5,685.80 | $11,371.60 | $.00 | $17,057.40 | 30.00 | $39,800.60 | $1,705.74 |
| Invoice Total = | $467,000.00 | $6,602.25 | $473,602.25 | $128,999.80 | $131,527.16 | $0.00 | $260,526.96 | 55.01 | $213,075.29 | $26,052.69 |

## CONTRACTOR'S APPLICATION FOR PAYMENT

Application is made for payment, as shown below, in connection with the Contract. Continuation Sheet is attached.

| | | |
|---|---|---|
| 1. | Original Contract Sum | $467,000.00 |
| 2. | Net Change By Change Orders | $6,602.25 |
| 3. | Contract Sum To Date (Line 1 +/- 2) | $473,602.25 |
| 4. | Total Completed And Stored To Date | $260,526.96 |
| 5. | Total Retainage | $26,052.69 |
| 6. | Total Earned Less Retainage (Line 4 Less Line 5 Total) | $234,474.27 |
| 7. | Less Previous Certificates For Payment (Line 6 from prior Certificate) | $116,099.82 |
| 8. | Current Payment Due | $118,374.45 |
| 9. | Balance To Finish, Including Retainage (Line 3 less Line 6) | $239,127.98 |
| | Current Payment Subtotal (Line 8) | $118,374.45 |
| | Current Payment Tax | $0.00 |
| | Current Payment Total | $118,374.45 |

| Change Order Summary | Net Change |
|---|---|
| Previous Invoices | $0.00 |
| This Invoice | $6,602.25 |
| Total | $6,602.25 |

With the completion-based payment method, the work-completed percentage can be subjective—is plumbing really 65 percent complete or only 40 percent? There's a tendency for the completion percentage to be overstated by a contractor in order to get payments sooner. It often equals out in the end since you don't pay the contractor immediately—typically a week and a half to three weeks after receiving a payment application. By that time, the work-completion percentage has likely met or exceeded estimates.

A common point of owner confusion or frustration involves seeing payment applications for supposed work completed when nothing has been installed. It's important to understand that part of "work completed" involves subcontractors' purchase of materials or off-site construction. A perfect example is millwork. Let's say you see millwork billed at 80 percent complete, yet a carpenter has never stepped foot in your store. How is this possible? Well, for your millwork to be installed tomorrow, raw materials were purchased many weeks ago. Then, carpenters spent weeks building the millwork in their shop. There's a good chance the millwork package is largely complete and the millworker is just waiting on the superintendent's go-ahead for a two-day installation.

Owners can be alarmed at sizable 10 percent or even 20 percent down payments requested by contractors before the commencement of construction. Understand that construction materials have lead times, sometimes requiring purchase many weeks in advance. To keep to a construction timeline, deposits on materials or rental equipment may be needed upon the execution of the GC's contract.

If a GC needs to install $40,000 worth of new HVAC rooftop units (RTUs) four weeks into construction, but the HVAC units have a seven-week lead time and require a 50 percent down payment upon placement of the order, those units need to be purchased before the start of construction.

We've all heard horror stories about clients paying a general contractor huge sums of money in advance of work commencement only to never again hear from the GC. Those instances are few and far between, but it's a tough pill to swallow when it happens to you. That's why you should always vet a general contractor (see "Contractor Vetting," above). If you're not sure why your GC requires money in advance, simply ask what the money is for, and follow up on those answers to confirm.

Once a GC issues a payment application (requesting money), you typically have 5 to 20 calendar days to pay. There's no industry standard for required payment timing; therefore it's up to negotiation during review of the construction contract. Anything less than five days can make it tough to pay on time, especially given that many banks require additional time to review large wire transfers.

If you're financing the project through an SBA loan or conventional loan where the lender pays the contractor directly, or if the bank releases only partial funds to you when a GC issues a payment application, request at least 10 days to pay your contractor, as lenders may have additional stipulations to sort through before releasing funds.

Whatever payment structure you use, *always* require that 10 percent retainage be paid to the GC only after all work, including punch list items, have been completed. (See A, B, C, of "Milestone-based payments" above.) This is an industry standard holdover percentage. If the contractor fails to redo subpar work or complete construction in a timely manner, you now have the ability to seek another contractor to finish the work, paying the new contractor out of the remaining 10 percent balance. Before seeking another contractor to finish your work, refer to your construction contract to make sure you're going about the situation properly.

As humans, we're good at starting projects but not necessarily good at finishing them. Requiring 10 percent retainage protects you, and better ensures that final construction items are completed expediently.

Regardless of how you structure payment schedules, base payments on tangible markers that connect to the progress of construction. *Do not* agree to payment structures tied to timetables, i.e., a predetermined amount due each month. Construction tends to be prolonged. You can quickly find yourself in a scenario where you've paid 90 percent of the contract amount, yet the construction completed is a mere fraction of that amount. That's not a fair deal. It puts you at risk and fails to incentivize builders to finish the project.

There's no industry standard for the number of draw payments or draw amount (or percentage). Draw quantities vary based on the length and the dollar amount of a project. The longer and more expensive a project, the more draw payments (resulting in smaller payment percentages). A $60,000 project that's 2 to 4 weeks long could entail just 2 or 3 payments, whereas a 30-week, $1.2 million project could require 10 or more payments. Your average retail or restaurant tenant improvement job with construction valued at $100,000 to $600,000 and anticipated 8 to 16 weeks to construct typically has 3 to 6 payments.

# PART 6: FURNITURE, FIXTURES, AND EQUIPMENT

**FF&E Selection**

When selecting equipment, it can be difficult to figure out what's good quality and what isn't. An internet search for equipment brands turns up many articles that are biased by dealers' representatives who exclusively sell a certain brand, writers who get paid for favorable product reviews, or customers who base their opinion on a single experience. Generally speaking, equipment warranties speak for themselves. The longer the parts-and-labor warranty, the better quality the item. Manufacturers peddling junk products aren't able to cover the high cost to warranty subpar equipment. High-quality refrigeration (Delfield, True, and Turbo Air, to name a few) can easily cost 50 percent more than their inexpensive counterparts, but their equipment is generally considered good quality, and their extended warranty coverage (typically three-year parts and labor, and five-year compressor coverage) speaks for itself.

When equipment that's under warranty breaks, you must first call a certified repairman who's an approved vendor of the manufacturer. If the equipment is deemed irreparable, you're usually on the hook for hauling away the broken equipment while you're waiting for a new unit. The time to fix or replace defunct equipment often parallels the price point of the product, meaning high-quality products typically have an abundance of parts in stock and a vast network of repairmen available seven days a week. It can take a week or longer to fix or replace broken equipment from "value brands" that don't have service programs as robust as their higher-end counterparts.

Is there equipment that's critical to your store's success, such that store operations would be crippled while you're waiting for repairs or replacement? Think point-of-sale (POS) systems, printing presses for graphics shops, hydraulic lifts for repair shops, or cooking equipment and refrigeration for food-service concepts. If your concept has critically important equipment, buy new, and don't skimp on quality. The financial losses incurred because of the breakdown of important store equipment is typically not worth what you save by buying used or from value brands.

You'll need to create your FF&E list during the beginning stages of your store's design. Although an equipment vendor may have the most extensive knowledge of price points, and pros and cons of different manufacturers or types of equipment, their opinion may be biased toward specific brands that they represent, equipment they need to offload, or financial kickbacks they receive from selling certain manufacturers' items. Consider seeking counsel from architects or consultants, who are great nonbiased sources.

When creating your FF&E list, try to use the same brands for items such as plumbing fixtures, lighting, refrigeration, and stainless steel (tables, sinks, faucets, and shelving). Purchasing FF&E piecemeal is taxing on whoever's paying the various vendors and tracking dozens of shipments with equipment arriving sporadically.

Once you've created an FF&E list, you have two options for purchasing: Purchase items yourself or hire an equipment contractor or KEC (kitchen equipment contractor). As implied, KECs typically work with people opening food-service concepts who have lots of equipment and smallwares. A KEC will take your list and create a single equipment quote. Given their volume annual purchasing, KECs often get deeper discounts than the general public. Depending on the level of service you desire, KECs can also coordinate the delivery of equipment as well as oversee the unpacking, setup, and start-up procedures for equipment. KECs usually provide a warranty booklet and work directly with manufacturers on swapping out any broken or defective equipment.

KECs won't provide costs for or facilitate the delivery of all your store's FF&E; small items such as pens and paper, construction materials, audio and electronics, and custom-manufactured goods are often excluded.

FF&E is often drop-shipped directly from manufacturers, so if you'd like the KEC to deliver all your store's equipment on a certain day, they must first direct your FF&E to a warehouse weeks in advance. When you're ready for everything, the KEC will put your FF&E on a truck and deliver everything to your store in one fell swoop. This costs a premium, but there's value to be had in this service because of the assured arrival of all equipment when your contractor needs it.

When ordering custom-built furniture or equipment, vendors typically want to get the order out the door the moment it is ready. Storage space is limited, and every square foot of a vendor's warehouse is valuable. You may incur hefty penalties from vendors who must house your order for extended periods of time (often over 30 days). This can add up to thousands of dollars in holding fees, so make sure you have a receival game plan for any specialty FF&E. Vendors have been known to "accidentally" ship orders before a client's requested ship date, presumably because their warehouse filled up.

**HVAC and Water Heaters**

This is bit different from equipment, but the common denominator in all retail spaces is an HVAC RTU (heating, ventilation, and air circulation rooftop unit) and a water heater. If you're going into a second-generation space, there will be an existing HVAC RTU or RTUs and a water heater. Consider having a service technician inspect the units to determine their current condition, how much more life the units are believed to have, and their age. If either of these systems breaks during your tenure, your store may need to close while repairs or replacements are made. Replacing an HVAC RTU can take many days, even weeks. Therefore, it's often best to start out with a new unit. As a general rule of thumb, you can count on water heaters to run for 8 to 10 years, and HVAC units for 8 to 12 years, although some systems are still going strong after 20 years in service.

There's *zero* consensus on the best HVAC brand to use. Most engineers and contractors are biased toward one of the seven main HVAC brands, with no consensus on any brand (Trane, Rheem, Goodman, Carrier, Nortek, Lennox, and York*). Spend 10 minutes online and you'll find that everyone has an opinion that one brand is better or worse than the rest. I argue it doesn't matter which HVAC brand you use for two reasons:

1. The Big Seven largely use the same guts—for instance, the condenser motors come from one of two suppliers (GE and Dayton), Copeland supplies most of the compressors, Sporlan makes almost all the thermostatic expansion valves, and so forth.
2. The mechanical contractor is paramount; arguably the most important factor is the mechanical contractor installing the equipment. The system is only as good as the workmanship performed by the installer. Equally important is the level of service the mechanical contractor provides. When it's 105 degrees outside and dozens of HVAC systems in your city fail, how long will it take the mechanical contractor who installed your system to get you back up and running? Two to three days or two to three weeks?

*There are dozens of HVAC brands, but they're almost all offshoots of the Big Seven.

**FF&E Receival Game Plan**

Get a game plan for the receival location and receival person for all owner-provided FF&E. Even if you bring a KEC on board, there will be items the KEC won't handle. Have these discussions with your contractor before signing the GC's contract. Shipping your equipment to the job site and just expecting the superintendent to manage receiving, unloading, and storing everything is a bear of a task, which contractors don't typically do for free. If you'd like the GC to manage receival of your FF&E, have those conversations during bid review to avoid project delays and change orders during construction.

Having FF&E shipped directly to the job site before the needed install date is generally not advised. Equipment tends to get damaged, lost, or stolen at job sites. It also gets in the way of the subcontractors' ability to complete their work. When this happens, they become frustrated, pushing boxes aside without regard to their contents. Smaller packages may get mistaken for trash and get thrown into the yardage bin. If the floors of your business need work done—whether it be staining and sealing concrete or laying tile and carpet—all FF&E will need to be moved for the floor subcontractors to do their work. Unfortunately, flooring installation often happens at the eleventh hour of construction. In this case, your equipment cannot go into the store until the last minute.

Now you're probably thinking, *I can beat the system by coordinating the arrival of all FF&E to be on-site right when it's needed.*

Good luck. In theory it sounds easy. In reality, a vendor's anticipated lead times and ship dates constantly change. They have seasonal demand swings, and "in stock" versus "out of stock" can drastically change lead times. To add more complexity, vendors don't have control of shipping, so once a product goes on a delivery truck, the vendor has no control over when the truck will deliver your package.

The big problem with trying to coordinate last-minute arrive of all your FF&E is that odds are high that something will arrive broken or missing, or the entirely wrong piece of equipment will arrive. If the wrong-color light fixtures arrived, or a sink comes broken and your GC needs to install it tomorrow, your project will be held up as the GC waits for the needed fixtures. To add insult to injury, a contractor may now be justified in issuing a change order for their additional time on the job site because of your equipment delays.

**FF&E Storage Location**

Where should you have your FF&E sent? Assuming you don't pay a KEC to manage delivery of your equipment, the best option is often to use an empty retail unit in your shopping center. Ask your landlord if anything is available. Make sure it's a secured unit. The next best bet is renting portable storage units. If you're a concept with a lot of FF&E (such as a restaurant), get multiple 40-footers. A 150-seat restaurant can fill up a single 40-footer with palletized chairs, tables, and table bases alone! Get landlord approval to place storage containers in their parking lot or garage. If your only option is street parking, you'll need city approval. If neither of the first two options work, ask your GC if they have a warehouse or storage facility. This is not as preferable, because any contractor's storage site will surely be a hike from your store, requiring receiving the equipment at the off-site facility, then hauling it across town.

When working with your FF&E vendors, make sure you have a game plan for receival of heavy items. Assuming you don't have a loading dock or forklift at your retail space, deliveries too heavy to lift will require a shipping truck with a liftgate. A liftgate is a hydraulic platform that can safely lower your equipment to the ground. Many vendors charge extra for liftgates, sometimes $50 to $150 per delivery, although it may be your only option.

**Used FF&E**

Businesses close their doors or upgrade equipment all the time. Because of this, there's an abundance of used FF&E that you can snatch up for pennies on the dollar. Most used equipment is just one to three years old, with a lot of life to go. Purchasing slightly used equipment means you may be covered under the original warranty, *if* there are original purchase receipts. In limited instances, used equipment will come with 30- to 90-day warranties by the reseller. Be warned: Any extended warranties will have limited warranty coverage, and 30–90 days is much less than the one- to three-year parts-and-labor warranty that you can expect on new equipment, so weigh all options when considering whether to purchase used.

Used equipment can be likened to buying a car. The day it's driven off the lot, the price depreciates dramatically, and there are deals to be had on well-maintained, slightly used equipment. Be cautious of buying used electronics or mechanical equipment without a 30-day money-back guarantee. At a minimum, a limited return warranty gives you enough time to discover any defects. Is the item being sold "as is"? If so, it doesn't hurt to ask for a 30-day money-back guarantee. Everything in life's negotiable. Speaking of negotiating, used equipment prices are rarely set in stone. Just as when you're purchasing a used car, don't be afraid to haggle!

There are a couple of avenues for acquiring used retail equipment:

1.  **Local resellers**—Some auctions occur at the actual location of the closed retail store. Others are at a liquidator's warehouse or showroom. You may have to pay an entry fee to enter auctions.

2. **Online resellers**—Online resellers usually have a wider selection of equipment than a local reseller, but be cognizant of shipping costs, which can add up quickly. This is a cost you won't incur when purchasing locally. When purchasing online, you won't be able to inspect FF&E before it arrives. Although items should be well photographed, when buying used, nothing beats being able to physically inspect the equipment!

3. **Direct peer to peer**—Sites such as Craigslist and Facebook are less common, but there are always people selling used FF&E on these platforms. This can be more laborious, because you're reaching out to individual users for single pieces of equipment, and sellers can be flaky. Since you're dealing with average Joes, not accredited companies, it can be the Wild West. Any purchases are "as is." Good luck finding the person for returns! Watch out for scammers, and always meet in a public place. All the potential hassle aside, purchasing directly from the source means you're knocking out a middleman and the additional costs that come with the middleman, so there are deals to be had!

Even if you're not a restaurant concept, consider doing an internet search for used restaurant equipment. There's a huge industry centered on reselling restaurant equipment. As such, you may be able to find dual-application FF&E such as plumbing fixtures, lighting, and furniture for your concept.

The deals extend beyond used equipment. When FF&E gets dinged during transit, it's generally cheaper for an equipment seller to mark down the price and sell it "as is" with cosmetic defects than to return it to the manufacturer for repairs. This is often referred to as "scratch-and-dent" furniture, fixtures, and equipment. If you're trying to save money but don't want to buy used, consider asking your equipment providers if they have any marked-down "scratch-and-dents." The cost savings can be as good as buying used!

## Substituting Equipment and Fixtures

You, your equipment provider, or architect will need to create an equipment schedule while plans are being produced. Since this happens early in a store's development, odds are good that any used equipment you're looking to purchase is not yet known. Your design professionals will need the specific make and model of equipment. Because of this, you'll likely need to specify new equipment.

Your design professionals need the exact make and model of equipment and fixtures to confirm they will fit in the floor plan as well as to draw in proper mechanical, electrical, and plumbing connections. Further, plan reviewers look over all equipment and fixture cut sheets to make sure items such as light fixtures conform to energy code, and plumbing fixtures meet water flow requirements.

Whether purchasing equipment new or used, *make sure what's purchased matches your plan's equipment schedule*. If any equipment deviates from what's declared on the plans, confirm that its footprint and any mechanical, electrical, or plumbing connections match what's shown on the plans. Too often equipment providers propose alternatives to what's shown on the plans because of cost or availability—or so they say. It's hard to see what's going on behind the curtains. Most equipment providers have deals to represent specific manufacturers' brands, getting kickbacks or discounts when selling a partner brand's equipment. Other times a dealer has excess inventory that they're just trying to offload. Sometimes equipment providers recommend a supposed like-for-like alternative for a cost savings. This makes them appear to be the "hero" saving you money, when in fact, they are proposing an inferior product (or lesser warranty) and pocketing a bigger savings on the alternative item than the savings you're getting. Many equipment vendors are reputable, but do your homework before accepting substitutes.

Given the various ways an equipment vendor can profit off providing alternative items, they don't always look into whether the equipment will match the footprint or mechanical, electrical, and plumbing specifications on your plans. If you accept an alternative item without doing research, *you* will be the person paying your contractor to make changes to accommodate the new equipment. Be cautious when substituting fixtures and equipment models that differ from what's shown on your plans!

**Unspecified Finishes**

As far as finish materials go, specifying a generic item will usually suffice, unlike equipment. Plan reviewers don't typically care what type of marble you're using, although your general contractor will not be able to provide an actual price on nonspecific materials until they know exactly what's desired. This can cause price discrepancies when a GC's estimated allowance amount for an unspecified material is over or under what was actually purchased and installed. In addition, unspecified loose ends have a tendency to be forgotten, which leads to project delays, so solidify all materials and finishes when plans are being produced!

**Properly Receiving and Inspecting Deliveries**

When FF&E is received, always check the condition of the container's contents before signing for the shipment. I can't remember a project where at least one shipment did not arrive damaged or there was a dispute over the contents of the delivery. *It happens all the time!* Never feel pressured by a waiting delivery driver when you're inspecting the shipment.

Always make sure the packing label on the side of a pallet adds up to what actually arrived. Just like airlines sometimes lose your luggage when you're traveling, delivery companies sometimes lose parts of an order in transit or vendors accidentally undership the order. Unlike losing your luggage, when you sign a delivery receipt, you're acknowledging that the delivery matches what's on the packing slip, and you won't be able to call the shipping company later to say a box is missing.

For orders that arrive damaged, you have two options:

1. Reject the shipment altogether, and refuse to sign for it.

2. Note the damages on the bill of lading (BOL), take photos of the damages, and then sign for the package. Make sure you get a copy of the BOL. Going this route is not advised, because signing for the package is an acknowledgment that you're receiving the delivery "as is."

Once you've signed for a delivery, the shipping company is usually off the hook for damages and missing items. The vendor is often also off the hook, although vendors are generally more willing to work with you so long as you contact them immediately after receiving a shipment. If goods need to be returned, you'll be on the hook for reboxing, scheduling shipping, and return shipping costs (unless the vendor is willing to provide a prepaid digital return label). Some suppliers will provide partial credits if you're willing to live with the dings and damages in lieu of returning the goods.

If you've elected to ship your store's FF&E to the job site, the on-site superintendent will need to sign for everything (or sometimes the signer is whatever worker the delivery driver first stumbles across). Make it clear to the superintendent how you expect them to receive deliveries.

Pro tip: Print written directions for how orders are to be inspected and signed for or rejected. Place the note next to the front door so expectations are crystal clear. Now when the superintendent signs for damaged packages, you can point to your sign and leave him to deal with remediating the situation.

Again, just about every project has items that show up broken or incomplete. If they're not properly dealt with, *you* will be on the hook for purchasing replacement goods or returning deliveries.

# PART 7: SIGNAGE

Even in this digital age, properly displayed storefront signage (your company name and logo over the front doors) is an incredibly valuable asset. Statistics show the majority of consumers patronize a store based on seeing its sign, not on word of mouth or through an online keyword search. A FedEx "What's Your Sign?" survey found that 76 percent of consumers entered a store they'd never visited based on seeing its sign. Sixty-eight percent of the consumers made a purchase because the sign caught their attention [14].

**Sign Considerations**

There's a lot of bad signage out there that detracts from businesses' ability to acquire customers. Follow these do's and don'ts to make sure you get your brand out to the world!

1. **Make it large and legible**—The paramount objective of signage is to display your store's name in a large and readable presentation. Passing motorists don't have three seconds to try to make sense of fancy cursive writing. Have your signage vendor produce the largest sign possible per any landlord restrictions and city code requirements.
2. **Keep objects to a minimum**—Because of landlord and city signage requirements, you have a finite space on the building's façade for your signage.

Adding objects to a sign often decreases the letter size, which decreases the overall visibility and readability of your store name.

3. **Be understandable**—If you're a restaurant named Ramsing, putting just that name on your storefront fails to convey that you're a restaurant and what type of restaurant. Sure, an astute passerby may be able to gather you're a restaurant by peering through the windows, but that's not good enough. You need to instantly showcase what you are by adding a tagline under ambiguous business names. Challenge yourself to keep the tagline to two words. For instance, Ramsing Taco Shop.

4. **Color contrast**—If your primary logo has red lettering, putting it directly onto a similarly colored backdrop such as a redbrick façade makes it difficult to read. There are tricks to the trade, such as bordering the letters in a contrasting color or adding a backboard in a different color. You may need to alter your logo from its standard color to effectively contrast with a building façade. Even the iconic green Starbucks logo can be found in white or black lettering based on the backdrop color it's up against. Remember, not everyone has 20/20 vision like you!

5. **Sign shape**—Consider a horizontal rectangular sign. They're easier to read, and some city sizing criteria favors horizontal rectangular signs over square, circular, and vertical signs.

**Signage Types**

There are three main types of signage:

1. **Traditional**—Signs that affix flat onto a building's façade are considered traditional storefront signs.
2. **Blade**—Blade signs protrude off a building's façade, hanging over the sidewalk. These are recommended in downtown or neighborhood settings where there's heavy walking traffic. Blade signs catch the attention of walking traffic better than traditional signs, which require passersby to crank their heads up and sideways to view. Blade signs are typically complementary (in addition) to traditional signs, not replacements for them.
3. **Monument or pylon**—These are structures at the turn-in of a shopping center that display all the center's tenant names. The words *monument* and *pylon* are often used interchangeably, although technically monument signs are no taller than 10 feet. Pylon signs can reach in excess of 100 feet tall. When working with your signage vendor, make sure they include quotes to produce slide-in inserts for your pylon sign (if your shopping center has such). Downtown shops without dedicated parking lots typically don't have pylon signs. Since pylon signage space is much smaller than storefront signage, readability is key. Keep pylon signage only to your store's name, no symbols.

**Signage Lighting**

Make sure your sign is lit, even if you're a 9-to-5 business! There are three way to light signage:

1. **External**—These typically use a gooseneck or spotlight fixture protruding from a building's façade (usually provided by the landlord).
2. **Internal front-lit**—Front-lit signs have a face made of fabric or an acrylic material that lets light shine through the material, illuminating the front of the sign.
3. **Internal halo-lit**—Halo-lit signs have a solid front and clear back, allowing internal light to illuminate the rear of the sign, creating a halo effect.

**Signage Materials**

Signs can be made from a multitude of materials: wood, metal, neon tubes, vinyl, plastic, and fabric, to name a few. A single sign will run you $500–$10,000, depending on its size, material, complexity, and quantity of colors. There are always exceptions to the rule. I've seen DIYers buy a $100 wooden butcher block, have their kid burn letters into it at their school's woodworking shop, then self-affix the sign to their business with $50 in brackets from the local hardware store. I've also seen signs hand-painted onto a building's façade for next to nothing.

A sign 9 feet long by 3 feet high by 5 inches thick, with 20 channel letters, LED backlighting, an acrylic face, and black painted aluminum sides and back will likely cost $3,000–$7,000, depending on your city, mounting details, the number of colors, and logo or letter complexity. This cost is a turnkey estimate for the vendor to acquire the signage permit, and manufacture and install the signage.

**Signage Styles**

These are the most common sign design styles:

1. **Channel**—With a channel sign, each letter or object of the sign is an unconnected individual piece. Channel signs are 3D. As you'll see in the below example, the sign is essentially made up of seven independent sign pieces.
2. **Box or cabinet**—The name is a literal reference to what the sign is. A box sign is an internally lit, flat-faced box or cabinet with graphics printed directly onto its front. A box sign is a singular unit and can be up to half the cost of a channel sign.
3. **Cloud**—A cloud sign is a happy medium between a box sign and a channel sign. Like a box, it's a singular unit. Unlike a box sign, the face is not flat; rather it's a 3D molding. Clouds cost more than boxes but typically less than channel signs.

**The Signage Process**

You'll need a permit from the city to install your signage. This process is handled outside of acquiring the general building permit, although the signage vendor should acquire the permit on your behalf. Start the process of acquiring your signage the moment you have a signed lease. The earlier you get your signage installed, the sooner you can capitalize on the marketing and exposure it provides.

Signage cost can vary considerably from vendor to vendor, so get two or three quotes. Different vendors can provide fresh perspectives on the type/quantity/style of signage. If you don't know who to bid the project to, here are a few ways to find vendors:

1. Ask your landlord for references. Your landlord may have a preferred vendor who has done work in your shopping center.
2. Ask neighboring tenants.
3. Do an internet search.

Signage vendors are a dime a dozen. There's no shortage of vendors!

Once you have bidders lined up, you'll need to send vendors the following:

1. A copy of your signage files
2. A copy of your lease. The vendor will look through your lease to see what parameters and stipulations your landlord has earmarked for signage.
3. A request that vendors provide their proposals with the maximum-sized sign allowable by local code and any landlord restrictions
4. Exterior elevations of the space. These documents can be found in your landlord's "as-built" plans. Without these, the vendor must come out to your space and survey the exterior building dimensions, which takes extra time (and sometimes additional costs).
5. Direction on quantities and placement of the signage. Some owners prefer a single sign over their entrance. If your store is visible to traffic from the rear of your business, consider adding signage to the back of your space. If you're in an end cap with side visibility, you may want a third sign on the building's end. If you're downtown, consider a blade sign. If you're not sure how many signs you want, ask that vendors provide à-la-cart pricing so

you can choose the style and quantity of signs that fit your budget.

6.  A request that vendors provide a turnkey proposal to acquire permits, manufacture the signage, and install the signage. The only thing signage vendors won't do is wire the sign. That must be done by a licensed electrician, i.e., it will be your GC's responsibility.

Pro tip: Most electrical engineers will make provisions to wire only a single sign over your store's entrance. If you have more than one internally lit sign, make sure to relay that information to your architect or engineer, so bidding GCs will include the appropriate signage wiring cost in their bid. This prevents change orders and project delays during construction.

Vendors typically send back a sample drawing showing the proposed design, placement, and different quantities of signage. Once you're happy with what's shown on their drawing, they will send corresponding pricing to match the agreed-upon design layout. At this point they should also provide more detailed "shop drawings," which should show signage schematics, attachment details, dimensions, materials, electrical specifications, and exact color codes.

**Local Versus National Signage Providers**

Like I said, there are a lot of signage vendors out there. You may have vendors preemptively reach out, looking for your business. Some of those vendors are out-of-towners. If you're with a franchise organization, your franchisor may have a program set up with a national preferred vendor.

Below are considerations to factor in when choosing between a local and national vendor.

- The signage provider must submit the signage proposal to the city for approval. Local providers are at an advantage over national providers since they'll often know the local code and process better. They may even have good rapport with the plan reviewer(s). Local vendors have in-house installers. Out-of-towners typically contract the work out to local install companies. This all leads to faster approval and installation of your signage when using a local company.
- For franchise organizations, local providers may be more expensive than the preferred national vendor, given that this is a one-off project for them. National vendors often provide competitive pricing based on doing multiple projects for an organization. With that said, the cost can be offset by high shipping costs, since they're likely shipping the signage from a regional manufacturing facility. This is a cost you don't incur when working with a local provider.

**Signage Vendor Selection**

Once you've received bids from vendors, you'll need to decide what provider to use. Before accepting a vendor proposal, it's perfectly acceptable to push for lower costs.

Make sure you're making an apples-to-apples comparison with the bids. One vendor may appear more expensive than the others if they add another sign, include the permit fee, or provide an extended warranty, when in fact their per-unit cost is lowest.

Once you've selected a vendor, remit payment to get the ball rolling and give them your general contractor's contact information for coordination of install. Send the GC a copy of the signage shop drawing so they know the electrical specifications to wire for.

# PART 8: CONSTRUCTION

**Construction Start Date**

Request a construction start date while you're reviewing and in the process of executing the GC's contract. If building permits have not yet been issued, see how soon the contractor can start after receiving permits. Some GCs can start immediately after contracts have been executed, but most need a week or two. Why? Once you contract with the GC, the GC in turn needs to contract with his subcontractors. Even if all the subcontractor paperwork is executed in short order, subcontractors may not be able to jump on a new project right away, especially in hot construction markets. Further, the GC needs to appoint a project manager and superintendent to manage the project. I allow up to two weeks' mobilization time, from inking of paperwork to commencement of construction. If the GC asks for longer, push back, because their commitment to take on your project is also a commitment to starting construction within a fair amount of time.

**GC Schedule**

Along with getting a GC start date solidified, you'll want to request a construction schedule (assuming building permits have been issued) that starts on or shortly after the execution of the contractor's contract. The GC's schedule should outline the construction start date, certificate of occupancy date, subcontractor work dates, pertinent inspection dates, and when the GC needs owner-provided equipment. Construction schedules are typically provided in Gantt chart format.

Here's the not-so-fun part of a construction schedule. A hard concept for many to grasp is that *the construction end date is a constantly moving target.* Unless you hit the lottery, the actual construction end date will differ from what was initially forecasted. With so many moving parts, and reliance on so many people, the end date is bound to change, usually creeping further out as construction progresses. Why? There could be a million reasons:

To complete a project without delays, you're reliant on a multitude of subcontractors, utility companies, and service vendors to complete their work on time. If one person fails to complete their work when needed, it affects other tradesmen or inspections. Inspectors must show up within 24 hours of inspections being called, *and* you must pass all of your dozens of inspections on the first go-round. You need perfect weather for the duration of construction, because productivity decreases when it's too hot or cold. Rain, wind, lightning, and snow delay the installation of certain items. Construction materials must make it on-site when they're requested, with nothing on back order or arriving broken. Subcontractors must install all systems flawlessly with zero issues during system start-ups.

Owners cannot make plan changes or material substitutions that will delay the project. Owners must also get all their FF&E on-site when it's needed. No unforeseen construction anomalies can pop up. You need a laser-focused GC to orchestrate subcontractors' work and inspections. Your architect's plans must be flawless. Contractors' RFIs must be answered immediately. No change orders affecting construction can come up.

What are the odds of a project being pulled off without a hitch? Maybe 0.1 percent. Regardless, the construction schedule is an important organizational tool for a contractor, and the dates are benchmarks that the contractor should strive to meet. A schedule is equally important for owners to know when they need to get equipment on-site.

GCs typically want the bulk of your equipment on-site when construction is approximately 90 percent complete. Let's say you're working off the original schedule from two and a half months ago that indicates furniture is needed on-site today. You get it to the job site as shown on the schedule, but over the past two and a half months, things have come up and the GC is three weeks behind. He now needs the furniture to be taken out of the store so he can lay down the flooring. Yikes. To avoid this, consider setting up a monthly e-calendar reminder to request a revised schedule from the contractor so you're always on the same page.

### Getting a Jump on Construction

If you have a GC locked in but still no building permits, considering looking into what work can be done unpermitted. If there's an existing concept in the space that needs to go, find out whether you can buy an "over-the-counter" demolition permit. After any demolition, the GC typically spends one to two weeks saw-cutting concrete (if the floor is already in) and laying in underground plumbing. In many cities, doing this work unpermitted is not technically allowed, but builders and inspectors may have an understanding that so long as you don't backfill dirt over the underground plumbing, cutting floor and laying pipe is acceptable.

I always get a temperature read from my contractor on whether we can get a jump-start on construction. Time is money, and knocking out a couple weeks' worth of construction while you're waiting for building permits can be a big value-add.

Word of caution: Whenever you do unpermitted construction, you run the risk of being fined. Maybe I'm just lucky, but I've never had a project fined by city officials so I can't speak to the repercussions firsthand, but I've heard stories. If the building department wants to throw the book at you, depending on the circumstances and what city you're building in, they may slap hefty fines on you, the GC, and violating subcontractors. The GC and his subs can lose their licenses, and the city can hold up the release of your building permit. Know what you can and cannot do, and understand the risk at hand.

### "For Construction" Drawings

Once permits are ready, ask your architect for the "For Construction" set of plans—also called the "final set" or "final revisions." These are the plan iterations that have been reviewed and accepted by the city, to which the architect and engineers have made changes based on city comments as well as any owner-requested changes.

To easily showcase changes, architects and engineers will draw clouds around all plan changes. In the below plan snippet, you can see a cloud around the hallway corridor. Clouding changes allows a contractor to quickly see what plan changes have occurred.

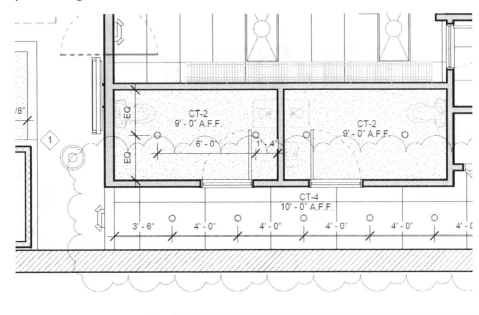

You can track changes by the plan log on the right-hand corner of each plan page. As you'll see below, the initial set of drawings was the "Permit" set that was logged into the city for building permits and sent to general contractors for bids. There were then multiple rounds of plan changes based on city and/or owner requests. The

11.4.18 drawings are the final set of plans that the contractor should build off.

| Issue Sets | | | | |
|---|---|---|---|---|
| No. | Issue Set | By | Date | Appr. |
| 1 | PERMIT | | 4.13.18 | |
| 2 | BLDG DEPT COMMENTS | | 7.20.18 | |
| 3 | BLDG DEPT COMMENTS | | 10.08.18 | |
| 4 | FOR CONSTRUCTION | | 11.4.18 | |
| | | | | |
| | | | | |
| | | | | |

Before sending the For Construction drawings to your contractor, make note of any changes between the Permit set of plans that the GC based his original bid on and the For Construction set. The contractor may need to increase his price based on plan additions or more expensive substitutes that were added. Conversely, you should be credited money back for any reductions in the scope of work or less expensive materials shown in the For Construction plans. Below is an example email:

*Mark,*

*Attached are the For Construction plans based on city comments. Please build off these plans. Any plan changes believed to warrant a change order must be presented to me within 5 business days from this notice.*

*As you'll see on the mechanical sheets, we've changed the RTUs to less expensive units. Also, the city would not let us use metal base cove, so we substituted a less expensive rubber base cove. Please issue a proposed credit amount for these items.*

*Best,*

Make sure your AIA construction contract references every plan page and plan page date, so that you and the contractor both know exactly which plan iteration the construction numbers are based on.

When walking through the construction site, make sure the plans you're looking at are the For Construction set. It never ceases to amaze me how often contractors fail to build off the latest set of plans. It's an epidemic!

If only a couple pages of the construction documents have been revised, to save money and paper, some GCs will do a page "slip" where they'll staple or tape new pages over only the pages that have changed. This is fine.

Some well-polished franchise organizations or on-the-ball architects will ask that different plan iterations be printed on different-color paper. To do this, the architect will add a sheet note onto every page of the Permit set of plans with large text that says,

"THE 'PERMIT' PLANS SHOULD BE PRINTED ONLY ON RED PAPER. THE 'FOR CONSTRUCTION' PLANS SHOULD BE PRINTED ONLY ON BLUE PAPER."

This practice makes it easy to distinguish which plan iteration is being used.

## Utility Meters

Upon the commencement of construction, do a site walk of your building complex, making note of existing utility meters for water, electricity, and gas—assuming your store uses gas. Any meters believed to be missing can be confirmed via the landlord's representative, your general contractor, or local utility company.

What's a meter? It's a device that measures incoming water, electricity, or gas. Utility companies use the consumption reading to bill customers for their proportionate amount of utilities. You won't be able to connect to a service's main connection point, or "tap spot," without a meter.

Unfortunately, utility companies are slow to install meters. They generally require a filled-out application, followed by a deposit payment. After both have been received, the utility company will put in a work order request for a local crew to schedule the installation. The entire process generally takes two to four weeks, and only utility companies can install meters. Identify what meters you may need, and then call your utility company to start the installation process upon the commencement of construction to avoid delays.

Gas is the most common meter requiring installation. If you're going into a first-generation space, odds are good you need a gas meter (assuming your business uses gas). Ask your architect or plumbing engineer if you're unsure whether your business requires gas.

Gas lines are made of brass, copper, or steel. Gas pipes are generally within 12 inches of an exterior wall. If the pipe has yellow wire wrapped around its end, it's likely gas. If there's a meter existing, it usually says "Gas," "Propane," or "Natural Gas" right on the meter. Gas meters come in different shapes and sizes, although the below example shows a business with a "typical"-looking gas meter. Also note that whereas the business on the left already has their meter installed, the right business has only a utility stub-up and needs a meter.

Just because you see a meter or meter bank doesn't mean it's yours! If you can't trace the gas line to your retail unit, odds are good it belongs to another tenant.

Having a meter doesn't mean it's sufficient. Depending on the gas loads indicated on your plans, an existing meter may need to be upsized—requiring a change in parts or a new meter altogether. Consult with the utility company to confirm you're good to go!

Follow the same steps to determine whether you have existing water and electric meters, and whether the current meters are sufficient. The common denominator among all meters, no matter the utility, is that they have analog or digital numbers to record consumption.

In addition to setting up your gas, water, and electricity accounts, don't forget wastewater and garbage.

Although your contractor will provide a yardage bin for construction debris, it's not for your use. I've seen GCs issue change orders to owners who fill up the contractor's yardage bin with boxes and packaging. If you elect to self-install equipment, dispose of the refuse yourself, or you may pay the price and piss off your contractor in the process!

Before setting up garbage disposal service, work with your landlord or review your lease to see whether the landlord provides common-area refuse, paid via your common-area maintenance fees.

### Wastewater

Some cities make setting up wastewater accounts easy by including payment under the water company. When the water and wastewater accounts are combined, the wastewater cost is generally a fluctuating rate based on water usage. Sometimes wastewater is a separate entity and service in which the bill is a fixed monthly rate. To find out, start by calling your water department.

### Mailbox Keys

Now that you've set up utility services, you've likely elected to have any paper bills sent to your business's mailbox. Where is your business mailbox, and how do you access it? Sometimes it's a mail slot in or near the front door of your business. Other times it will be in a cluster of mailboxes in your retail center. In limited instances, you must pick up your mail at a post office box. Ask your landlord's representative where mail is distributed and how to get your mailbox key.

**Owner and Contractor Coordination**

You'll need to work in tandem with your contractor to get your vendors' equipment and services set up. During weekly on-site meetings, make sure you know what upcoming items the GC needs you to work on, such as the following:

1. Determining finishes
2. Draw payments
3. Equipment delivery
4. Utility service setup
5. Coordination of owner's vendors
6. Addressing RFIs or outstanding change orders

As you can see, the contractor relies on the owner for a multitude of items to keep construction on pace. For example, if your space needs a gas meter, waiting until the last minute to call the utility company will surely delay the project. Failure to have the meter installed on time constrains the contractor's ability to test anything running on gas (HVAC, water heaters, and cooking equipment). Further, the contractor cannot get through final inspections without demonstrating working systems.

If project delays are owner derived, the contractor has the right to issue a change order for their extra time on the project—with the dollar amount typically a continuation of the GC's weekly general conditions costs and overhead and profits (OH&P). Let's assume throughout the project there's been a total of two weeks' worth of project delays directly attributed to the owner. The initial construction contract was $250,000 with a quoted 10-week build-out. The general conditions costs was $32,000 (or $3,200 per week). This is for costs such as scissor lift rentals, use of a portable toilet, mobile phones, and costs for a superintendent and project manager. The GC also charged $25,000 in OH&P (or $2,500 per week), because they're not doing the work for free. Now that the GC must keep all of their equipment and labor on-site for an additional two weeks because of owner delays, they're in the right to send you a change order to the tune of **$11,400**:

(($32,000 + $25,000)/10 weeks) x 2 weeks = $11,400

Refer to your construction contract for specifics on owner delays. As you'll see from the above example, all things being equal, the change-order dollar amount for delays should be a continuation of the initial contract cost. A GC who charges 10 percent in overhead and profits for the base construction cost but 18 percent in change orders is price gouging you, and you should fight back on the change-order amount.

**Owner Changes**

Be mindful of making changes or additions to the plans after they've been completed. Requesting plan changes can cause confusion and project delays. An innocent request such as swapping one toilet model for another can be tough on a contractor. A good contractor will have ordered long-lead-time items, such as the toilet, well in advance of the intended installation date. Now he must work with his plumber to see if the item has already shipped. If so, they must coordinate return of the fixture while confirming they can get the new fixture by the required installation time. Then there are the cost adjustments. If the new toilet is more expensive and the plumber doesn't feel like absorbing the cost, he will issue a change order to the contractor, who will in turn issue a change order to you. This all takes time and energy, ultimately detracting from a contractor's time that could be better spent managing subcontractors or pertinent project details. Imagine what happens to projects where owners make a dozen changes.

Even if you request changes to finishes or fixtures, *and* receive a confirmation from the contractor on acceptance of those changes, they don't always get implemented. Why?

1. **Poor communication**—If it's not in writing, there's a tendency for things to fall through the cracks. If you asked for a change while on-site or on the phone, follow up with an email. This creates a paper trail to refer to. Make sure you're clear with your requests. If you want something changed, ask for it. Don't just say, "Blue pendants would be nice."
2. **Failure to follow through**—Plan changes are typically distributed from the project manager to the on-site superintendent, then to the subcontractor's estimator, and finally to the subcontractor's laborers. If one person in the chain doesn't get the information, they'll end up building to the original plans.

3. **Workers build off the plans**—If changes don't make it onto the plans, odds are, your store will be built to what's shown on the plans. You can pay the architect to make the necessary plan changes, at which point they must be printed and overlaid onto the on-site plans. This takes time and money, so if the changes are not technical in nature, considering drawing the changes by hand onto the on-site plans.

What's the takeaway? Spend the extra time to review material and finish selections *before* plans get distributed to contractors! Making changes during the bid process or construction is frustrating for all involved.

It's important that you're happy with your store's design, so if you want something changed, do it. But also know when to let the small stuff go. Too many changes *will* create chaos, confusion, and project delays, and drive everyone mad in the process.

**Construction Site Meetings**

Upon the commencement of construction, on-site meetings should occur between the contractor's project manager, superintendent, and client (and sometimes the architect or consultant). These meetings are typically weekly. Site meetings allow for visual inspection of progress and facilitate better communication. These face-to-face meetings help build trust and allow for nonverbal expressions such as a nod of assurance or smile that can create consensus. In-person communication also avoids the pitfalls of emails and texts that can be misinterpreted.

It's nice to have the GC email an itinerary or overview of pertinent meeting items to the necessary parties in advance of the meeting. I've been to quite a few on-site meetings that were hastily prepared for, or half-assed. Requesting a meeting itinerary better assures that all parties will come prepared, including you.

The below items should be discussed at the site meeting, with meeting minutes promptly distributed afterward. Meeting minutes create a paper trail of events for any future dispute resolution and allow for project updates to be distributed to consultants, architects, business partners, lenders, or landlords who may need to be in the loop.

1. Work completed
2. Work in progress
3. Upcoming work
4. Outstanding owner items
5. Outstanding contractor items
6. Upcoming owner items
7. Upcoming payments
8. Record of subcontractors on-site
9. GC to communicate project status as "on schedule," "at risk," or "behind schedule." If "at risk" or "behind schedule," an action plan is required.
10. Meeting minutes

Projects are prolonged because issues are not dealt with swiftly. Find solutions to issues or roadblocks as expediently as possible.

**Change Orders**

Construction isn't a science. Because of this, change orders exist. A change order is a notice from the GC requesting additional money to complete the project. Change orders also come in the form of credits back to an owner. Common reasons for change orders include the following:

1. Miscommunication between the owner and contractor about who's supplying project materials or equipment
2. Items missing from the plans
3. Failure of the owner or owner's vendor to provide equipment or complete work on time, resulting in prolonged project time by the general contractor
4. Failure of the owner to make material selections on time
5. Owners substituting less expensive materials for costlier items
6. Owners asking that additional items be added to the contractor's scope of work
7. Contractor's or subcontractor's failure to walk the space during the bid process and properly identify existing conditions
8. Unforeseen items becoming apparent during construction
9. Hidden items being revealed after demolition
10. Changes required by city inspections during plan review or construction
11. Weather

These items constitute the bulk of change orders, although there are many more reasons for change orders, even on seemingly simple projects.

Change orders are often technical in nature, obfuscating, or interpretational. Consider having the architect or consultant review change orders to determine whether they're just and the cost is fair. Having reviewed many change orders over the years, I've been able to get clients out of unsubstantiated change orders, found no-cost work-arounds, identified opportunistic price-gouging, and negotiated costs down.

Contractors should submit change orders on an American Institute of Architects or equivalent change-order form for you to view. The change order should provide full information about the reason for the change order, cost amount, and any effect on the project schedule as a result of the change order. Change orders are not valid until signed by the client and contractor.

**Change Orders: Trust but Verify**

So often I hear . . .

"I just got a change order because the architect screwed up on X" or "I got a change order because the architect didn't add such-and-such to the plans!"

Before long, the GC and owner are best friends, and the architect is the enemy. Please dig a little deeper before paying that change order or sending a nasty note to the architect. Quite truthfully, the architect is an easy scapegoat. By the time construction begins, you're communicating with the contractor on a frequent basis, not the architect. It's inevitable that problems will pop up during construction. Instead of taking ownership for those mishaps, sometimes contractors will throw the easy target—the architect—under the bus, even when the problems may be a direct result of the GC's or subcontractors' negligence.

Investigate the situation before signing off on change orders or assigning blame. This involves a thorough review of all plans or contracts, which can get technical and may be best reviewed by a consultant or architect. Ethically your consultant is your fiduciary and your architect is required to support their set of documents, so don't be afraid to ask their opinion about a change order or to review it in full before you sign off.

Many change orders are avoidable and covered by the minute "CYA" notes that architects and engineers have within their plans that the GC is required to adhere to.

Let's review a real-world example with illustrations:

Your contractor claims the architect did not add office outlets for equipment to plug into. He flips to an electrical drawing and points at all the outlet locations, which shows outlets absent in the office (an outlet is indicated by two dashes running through a circle). To add the needed outlets, the GC has issued a change order for $3,800.

There's too much information for all plan details to go onto a single page, which is why plans take up multiple pages. You'll need to thoroughly inspect the plans, seeing if there's a reference note to view additional electrical details on another page or if one of the sheet notes specifies wiring of the office.

Upon initial inspection, the GC's claims appear true. But you're smart and know to investigate the situation further.

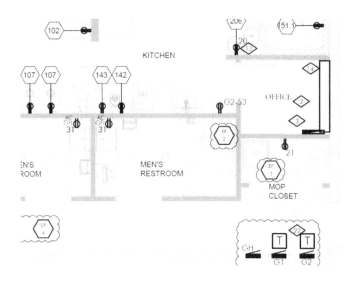

You see diamond numbers in the office area, indicating you must hunt for the corresponding diamond numbers 2, 3, and 14 for further information.

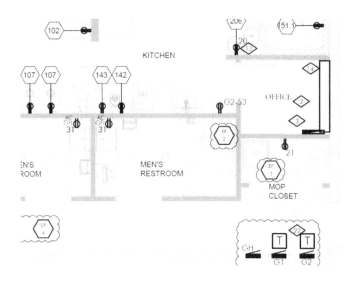

◇#◇ POWER PLAN KEYED NOTES:

1. SHOW WINDOW - PROVIDE FLUSH MOUNTED DUPLEX OUTLET IN CEILING OR WALL WITHIN 18" MAXIMUM ABOVE STOREFRONT FOR SHOW WINDOW LIGHTING IN ACCORDANCE WITH NEC 210.62.

2. TELEPHONE BOARD LOCATION (TTB) - THE E.C. SHALL PROVIDE AND INSTALL ¾"x12"x12" PLYWOOD BACKBOARD, INSTALL TIGHT TO CEILING AND PAINT TO MATCH WALL. PROVIDE 1"C WITH PULL STRING BACK TO THE BUILDING TELEPHONE/ DATA SERVICE ENTRANCE. PROVIDE DEDICATED NEMA 5-20R RECEPTACLE +84"AFF ON TTB AND CIRCUIT AS SHOWN. FIELD VERIFY LOCATION, MOUNTING HEIGHT AND ORIENTATION AND ADDITIONAL REQUIREMENTS WITH TENANT PRIOR TO BID OR ANY WORK.

3. REFER TO DETAIL 2/E1.0 FOR MANAGERS DESK RECEPTACLES AND CIRCUITS.

4. PROVIDE J-BOX WITH 5 PORTS FOR DATA CONNECTIONS INSIDE COOLERS. PROVIDE WITH 1" CONDUIT WITH PULLSTRING BACK TO MANAGER'S DESK.

Finding diamond note 3, it refers you to view detail 2 on plan page E1.0.

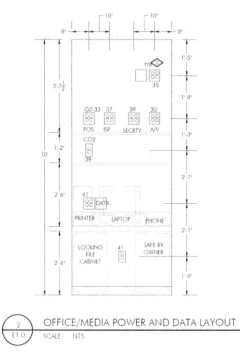

2
E1.0
OFFICE/MEDIA POWER AND DATA LAYOUT
SCALE: NTS

Flipping to page E1.0 you find detail 2. Sure enough, all the outlets are there!

| PANEL SCHEDULE: | | | G2 | | | | | | | | May 11, 2018 |
|---|---|---|---|---|---|---|---|---|---|---|---|

PROJECT:  
LOCATION: Back of Tenant Space  
JOB NO.: 2018-034  
COMMENTS: New Panelboard  

VOLTAGE L-L: 208  
VOLTAGE L-G: 120  
SYSTEM: 3Ø, 4-WIRE  

BUS RATING: 200A  
MAIN O.C. DEVICE: 150A M.C.B.  
MOUNTING: RECESSED  

S.C.RMS RATING: 10,000 AIC

| CIR NO. | AMPS | POLE | CONNECTED LOAD (VA) | NEC DEMAND FACTOR | DESCRIPTION OF LOAD SERVED | PH-A | DESCRIPTION OF LOAD SERVED | NEC DEMAND FACTOR | CONNECTED LOAD (VA) | POLE | AMPS | CIR NO. |
|---|---|---|---|---|---|---|---|---|---|---|---|---|
| 1 | 20 | 1 | 900 | 1.00 | Bar Conv. Receptacles | | Kitchen Recept | 1.00 | 540 | 1 | 20 | 2 |
| 3 | 20 | 1 | 900 | 1.00 | Table Conv. Receptacles | | Shunt Trip | | | | | 4 |
| 5 | 20 | 1 | 1000 | 1.00 | Heat Trace | | K133 Soda Machine | 0.65 | 180 | 1 | 20 | 6 |
| 7 | 20 | 1 | 1800 | 0.65 | X306 Ice Machine | | K140 Reach-In Ref. | 0.65 | 636 | 1 | 20 | 8 |
| 9 | 20 | 1 | 1450 | 0.65 | K307 Water Disp. | | K162 Gas Range | 0.65 | 180 | 1 | 20 | 10 |
| 11 | 20 | 1 | 180 | 1.00 | Bar Recept | | K141 Reach-In Freezer | 0.65 | 636 | 1 | 20 | 12 |
| 13 | 20 | 1 | 360 | 1.00 | Bar Recept | | Kitchen Cooler Comp. | 0.65 | 2364 | 2 | 20 | 14 |
| 15 | 20 | 1 | 180 | 1.00 | Bar Recept | | Kitchen Cooler Comp. | 0.65 | 2364 | 2 | 20 | 16 |
| 17 | 20 | 1 | 840 | 0.65 | K142 Food Processor | | Kitchen Freezer Comp. | 0.65 | 2364 | 3 | 25 | 18 |
| 19 | 20 | 1 | 216 | 0.65 | K143 Shear | | Kitchen Freezer Comp. | 0.65 | 2364 | 3 | 25 | 20 |
| 21 | 20 | 1 | 180 | 1.00 | Kitchen POS | | Kitchen Freezer Comp. | 0.65 | 2364 | 3 | 25 | 22 |
| 23 | 20 | 1 | 180 | 1.00 | Router | | Spare | | | 1 | 20 | 24 |
| 25 | 15 | 1 | 1020 | 1.00 | FC-1 | | Spare | | | 1 | 20 | 26 |
| 27 | 15 | 1 | 1020 | 1.00 | FC-2 | | K107 Cooktop | 0.65 | 1400 | 1 | 20 | 28 |
| 29 | 15 | 1 | 1020 | 1.00 | FC-3 | | K107 Cooktop | 0.65 | 1400 | 1 | 20 | 30 |
| 31 | 15 | 1 | 1020 | 1.00 | FC-4 | | MUA-1 | 1.00 | 576 | 3 | 15 | 32 |
| 33 | 20 | 1 | | | Spare | | MUA-1 | 1.00 | 576 | 3 | 15 | 34 |
| 35 | 20 | 1 | | | Spare | | MUA-1 | 1.00 | 576 | 3 | 15 | 36 |
| 37 | 20 | 1 | | | Spare | | KEF-1 | 1.00 | 1320 | 3 | 15 | 38 |
| 39 | 20 | 1 | | | Spare | | KEF-1 | 1.00 | 1320 | 3 | 15 | 40 |
| 41 | 20 | 1 | | | Spare | | KEF-1 | 1.00 | 1320 | 3 | 15 | 42 |
| 43 | 20 | 1 | | | Spare | | DF-1,2,3,4 | 1.00 | 672 | 1 | 20 | 44 |
| 45 | 20 | 1 | | | Spare | | Spare | | | 1 | 20 | 46 |
| 47 | 20 | 1 | | | Spare | | Spare | | | 1 | 20 | 48 |
| 49 | 20 | 1 | 360 | 1.00 | Greaser | | Spare | | | 1 | 20 | 50 |
| 51 | 20 | 1 | 180 | 1.00 | POS | | Spare | | | 1 | 20 | 52 |
| 53 | 20 | 1 | 180 | 1.00 | Kitchen Rec. | | Spare | | | 1 | 20 | 54 |
| 55 | 20 | 1 | | | Spare | | Spare | | | 1 | 20 | 56 |
| 57 | 20 | 1 | | | Spare | | Spare | | | 1 | 20 | 58 |
| 59 | 20 | 1 | | | Spare | | Spare | | | 1 | 20 | 60 |
| 61 | 20 | 1 | | | Spare | | Spare | | | 1 | 20 | 62 |
| 63 | 20 | 1 | | | Spare | | Spare | | | 1 | 20 | 64 |

CONNECTED LOAD:  
PHASE A (VA): 14,148  
PHASE B (VA): 12,114  
PHASE C (VA): 9,876  
TOTAL LOAD (VA): 36,138  

DEMAND LOAD:  
PHASE A (VA): 11,565  
PHASE B (VA): 9,399  
PHASE C (VA): 7,979  
TOTAL DEMAND LOAD (VA): 28,943    80.34 A

NOTES:

Further, you know that electricians price projects based on the type and quantities of circuits running to the electrical panel. For good measure, you flip to the panel schedule page and see that all the office outlets are properly shown. The electrician must have included the cost to wire the office, but if he didn't, the negligence is on his part and it is his cost alone to bear. You've determined that the change order is baseless and should be rejected.

The takeaway: Dig deeper before accepting change orders or accusing someone of fault. There may be more to the story.

### Change Orders—Receiving Credits

178

When it comes to change orders, the pendulum swings both ways! If it is found that items the GC originally budgeted for aren't needed, or if the GC asks to use cheaper material substitutes, make sure to get credited for the cost savings. Contractors are often quick to request additional money but can be slow or reluctant to issue credits.

When a contractor asks to use cheaper materials or forgo certain installations, *always* request a proposed credit amount *before* determining whether to accept those changes. Say the contractor asks to use metal-clad (MC) electrical conduit instead of the electrical metallic tubing (EMT) conduit that your plans call for. MC conduit is cheaper overall (because the installation process is much faster). You decide to accept the change in materials, and at the same time, request a credited amount from the contractor. A week later the GC gets back to you that the cost savings is only $200. By this time, installation of the MC conduit is complete. The cost savings should be many times this amount, but you've already agreed to the alternative material, which makes your ability to negotiate a better price an uphill battle. If you were to decide the cost savings isn't worth the change in materials, you'd actually be on the hook to pay the contractor to switch back to EMT conduit, since you already agreed to the change.

When a GC asks to use alternative materials but says there's no cost savings to the owner, rather "It's just a better way to build it," that might be true, but odds are decent they're requesting changes to save cost or time (and time is money). Those are cost savings that should go to the owner. Trust but verify. Research the situation before accepting any deviation from the plans, and get an opinion from your architect or consultant. *Always request a proposed credit amount before accepting changes.* This protects you and gives you a degree of negotiating leverage.

Side tangent: What are the downsides to using the cheaper MC conduit in lieu of EMT conduit? They're both fine, but MC conduit is an all-in-one electrical wire *and* conduit, whereas EMT is an independent conduit that different wires can sit in. If you decide to make changes to equipment with different electrical specifications down the road, with EMT, you can leave the conduit in place and simply pull out the old electrical wire, then "fish in" new wire. With MC conduit you must replace both the conduit and the electrical wire. So although EMT is slightly more expensive to install, electrical changes down the road are cheaper.

# PART 9: FINAL INSPECTIONS AND STORE OPENING

### Final Inspections and Certificate of Occupancy

As construction comes to an end, an important milestone is passing final inspections. After all final inspections are passed, you'll receive a certificate of occupancy (CO or CofO—it gets confusing because CO is also common lingo for change orders!). A CO allows you to occupy your retail space for more than just construction purposes—i.e., to run your business. There's typically a scorecard on-site near the front door that applicable inspectors must sign off after their respective inspections. Once you've passed all inspections, the contractor will take the scorecard down to the building department to apply for a CO. Depending on your jurisdiction, some COs are issued immediately. Other jurisdictions require a week (or more) for the scorecard to move through the clerical process before issuance of a certificate of occupancy.

If you fail an inspection, but the inspector deems the cause of failure not critical to health or safety, they may issue a temporary certificate of occupancy (TCO or temp CofO). A

TCO allows you to occupy the space, but you must reinspect (and pass) any failed inspections within a prescribed time frame. Acquiring a TCO and then failing to pass reinspection can carry fines or the loss of the TCO. To be eligible for a TCO you must often (but not always) pass required inspections such as electrical and fire marshal inspections.

What happens if you're caught occupying a space without a CO or TCO? It depends on the jurisdiction and how nice the city officials are. Sometimes it's a stern warning. Those less fortunate face fines, delays in receiving the CO/TCO, court-ordered sanctions, and the loss of certain insurance coverages or increased insurance rates [15].

**The Untold Truth About Passing Inspections**

How long will it take you to pass final inspections? Most GCs budget one to three days. Unfortunately, it rarely goes that fast. I analyzed 30 different tenant improvement projects spread throughout the country. The mean anticipated time was 2.2 days. The actual mean time was 11.4 calendar days—almost five and a half times as long! Why the disconnect? A couple of reasons. First, when choosing a GC, if one contractor says it will take two weeks to pass final inspections, and another closely priced contractor says two days, guess which one you're going to use?

There's also the "wishful thinking" factor from the GC. If all goes according to plan, you can technically get through inspections in two days. For that to happen, though, all subcontractors must substantially finish their work at the same time. Then, all inspectors must be available to immediately inspect the work. If that's not miraculous enough, all inspectors must sign off on their initial final inspection. Oh, and most cities have inspection prerequisites—i.e., you cannot call for one final inspection without passing another. See how improbable it sounds when you work through the equation? The takeaway: Don't bet on passing final inspections in two days.

**Scheduling Opening Dates**

What's one of the biggest mistakes that nearly every retail owner makes? Scheduling an open date too early. It's a costly and painful mistake. The tough thing to understand is that a GC's schedule is not gospel. Far from it. If anything, it's a rosy projection of events that assumes everything will go right: All subcontractors will finish their work on time, there won't be any weather issues, supply deliveries will be seamless, no unforeseen construction issues will arise, the architectural plans are perfect, owner-provided equipment arrives on time, inspectors come when they're supposed to *and* sign off on every inspection on the first go-round, and so on and so forth. You get the point. Unfortunately, construction doesn't work like that. With hundreds of moving parts and dozens of actors involved, it takes a lot for everything to go right but little for things to go wrong. Understand that the construction end date is an ever-moving target—with a tendency to creep outward.

This is how most projects go:

You schedule your store's opening date months in advance. The media publishes articles with the announced opening day. You do the same with your website and Facebook page. Now everyone knows when to come.

T-**minus** two weeks to store opening:

You've hired managerial staff and interviewed prospective employees who will be quitting their current jobs in a week and a half to come work for you. Opening inventory orders have been scheduled (possibly with perishable goods). Your marketing campaign distributes promotions with the opening day listed. You've scheduled a grand opening entertainer. Your parents have booked plane tickets from Kalamazoo.

T-**minus** one week to store opening:

It's become apparent the GC is behind. Inspections were supposed to take two days, but it's been a week, and so far, a few inspections have been postponed because subcontractors are behind. One inspector never showed up, and another inspector failed the HVAC inspection because there are no economizers.

*What the hell is an economizer?* you ask yourself.

The electrician took you off temporary power yesterday and fired up your systems, but breakers keep popping. Oops. He needs to rewire a few things before calling for electrical inspections. The internet provider is a week out from installation.

It's becoming apparent the GC needs another week or two, maybe more. Meanwhile your opening orders have been delivered to the store. The flooring subcontractor needs everything out so they can stain and seal the concrete floor in the back and install carpet in the front.

"Everything out," you scream. "TO WHERE?!"

T-**plus** one week of the store's opening:

Fast-forward two weeks. The big day was supposed to be last week, and I'm not talking about your wedding. This is bigger! Customers were showing up even though you scrambled to revise the open date on your website and Facebook. You've spent your remaining time working with your marketer to promote a new opening date. The entertainer is booked the rest of the month and can't make it. Dad's mad he can't make it; he's got a meeting in Kalamazoo he can't reschedule at the last minute. The employees are worried. They quit their jobs based on *your* assured opening date. They're desperate to start making some money.

Blown ego and pride aside, you're exhausted from rescheduling everything. You don't even want to add up the financial cost. But wait! There are ongoing issues with final inspections and construction, even though your GC assured you he'd be ready this time. Here we go again...

T-**plus** two weeks of the store's opening:

*Finally*, a week later you've passed all inspections. You're opening tomorrow, but since you spent the past three weeks scrambling to reschedule, then reschedule again, you're woefully underprepared and burned out. There are some construction punch list items outstanding, but you need to get your doors open. All those potential employees? Half took other jobs. The other half are irked. You're understaffed and need to restart the interview process when you have a minute. With your time spent elsewhere, there was no time for training. Baptism by fire for the employees and manager! You know there are issues with your merchant services, point-of-sale system, staff schedule, uniforms, employee paperwork, and opening orders, but there's no time to fix it now.

The next day, you open! You've poured your life savings and a thousand hours into the development of your store. What do you have to show for your efforts? A new store that has no business being in business. Customers will encounter an inexperienced and unhappy staff. Kinks are yet to be worked out, and construction loose ends remain. First impressions last a lifetime. Yikes. You're a smart person, so how did this happen? *You scheduled your opening day too early.*

Surely this is an overly dramatic worst-case scenario, right? Not even. This routinely occurs when you schedule an opening date in advance of work completion. So how should you schedule an opening date? For starters, keep dates vague for media and marketing. Never commit to a certain date, or even a hopeful date. People cling to dates. You could say, "We hope to open in the fall," or even "We anticipate an October opening." Don't say things like "We'll be open for the annual art show" or "We open October 1." If you've hired a marketer, they probably won't like the fuzzy window. Oh well.

Hold off on setting your opening date until you've completed all major construction, received a certificate of occupancy, and set up or installed necessary FF&E and services. By the end of construction, you'll have watched money go out the door for too long and you'll be hungry to start seeing money hit the till. But you *must* wait and do it properly. Sure, you'll have a short time to schedule your opening, but it's a lot better than the alternative.

A two- to three-week latency period between the end of construction and a store's opening affords the necessary time to hire staff, conduct proper training, and tie up the many loose ends. People always discount just how much busywork there is between the end of construction and a store's opening. A latency or buffer period is critical to ensuring your business's success!

Rocky openings come with bad customer reviews. In this digital age, bad reviews will tank a business. A 2018 Consumer Review Survey found the following:

1.  *86 percent of consumers read reviews of local businesses (including 95 percent of people aged 18–34).
2.  *57 percent of consumers will use a business only if it has four or more stars.
3.  *91 percent of 18–34-year-old consumers trust online reviews as much as personal recommendations [16].

Needless to say, the first weeks open can make or break your concept. There's an old Yiddish saying about business: "The way it begins is the way it ends." Don't start off on the wrong foot!

**Soft Opening**

Pro tip: Go through a "soft opening" phase before your grand opening (or advertised opening date). The grand opening should be at least a week after the soft opening.

For a food-service concept, put it two and a half to four weeks out. This affords you and your staff ample time to iron out the kinks, learn the point-of-sale system and store technologies, and the big one: create team synergy.

This is the first time you're all working together. It takes time for a group to get into a rhythm. Hell, just learning everyone's name takes time. If it's somebody's first week on the job, it's easy to tell. Just imagine opening your doors to the public if it's *everyone's* first week on the job, even the manager. Yikes.

Going through a soft opening period also allows time to dial in on the proper staffing level. The retail industry has high employee turnover—as high as 81 percent annually [17]. Guess when turnover is highest? An employee's first few weeks. The running joke is that two weeks' notice is standard in white-collar work, but two hours' notice is plenty in retail. It's common for retail employees to start a job, then decide it's not for them, quitting with little or no notice given to management. Further, some employees will interview well but need to be let go. Finally (depending on marketing efforts), many grand openings are busy! You'll need a staff with on-the-job experience to properly handle the hectic day. Pre-opening training is no substitute for actual on-the-job experience.

**Work Guarantee**

You've been open a few months and your water heater breaks. Darn! That's going to be a costly repair bill! Time to find a plumber to fix it. But wait! You may be throwing your money away. Why? It's industry standard for contractors and their subcontractors to warranty their work for one year from the completion of construction. The one-year warranty should cover parts and labor. If not already included by your architect, make sure the necessary warranty verbiage is added to your plans. Since a contractor agrees to adhere to all plan specifications, this *should* cover you, but it doesn't hurt to also add it to the contractor's contract. See below verbiage:

> *All work shall be guaranteed for one full year from date of obtaining the certificate of occupancy. The contractor and his subcontractors shall replace all defective workmanship, equipment, and materials without additional charges to the owner.*

A contractor's refusal to agree to a one-year work guarantee is a sign that he doesn't believe the quality of his work will withstand the test of time. And quite truthfully, one year is a low bar. Work guarantees also mitigate against the use of subpar workmanship and materials by builders. When builders know they're on the hook for the first year's worth of repairs, they're more likely to build it right the first time.

**Punch Lists**

When the GC has obtained a certificate of occupancy, you're typically nearing project completion. This is when you should create a punch list. A punch list is a document outlining all items that need redress, are missing, or are work-in-progress items that need to be completed. Once you've created a punch list, send it to the general contractor. Make sure the GC is in agreement with your list, and then request a completion date for all work outstanding. Five to 10 business days is reasonable for most projects.

Punch list items are often entirely neglected or take many weeks to fully address. By the time a punch list has been produced, the general contractor's superintendent and project manager have likely moved on to another project, along with their subcontractors. This leaves your project out of mind and out of sight. Hold the contractor to completing outstanding work by a prescribed date. Above all, don't pay your contractor their final 10 percent until all punch list items have been properly addressed (among any other contract stipulations). Prolonged punch list items have been known to drive a man crazy.

Although punch lists are typically produced by the owner, they don't have to be. A good GC takes pride in his work, and upon request, some GCs will produce their own punch list. This allows you to pick up on items you didn't catch or don't have expertise in, such as millwork that's not caulked at the seams. If you can get a GC to create their own punch list, compare their list with yours. Getting a GC to create their own punch list can be an uphill battle, because you're asking them to take on more work and note their subcontractors' shortcomings.

When I create a punch list, the GC often wants to walk the space with me to review and discuss everything. That's fine—even preferred, since it gets everyone on the same page—but I've found that to do a punch list right, you must go room to room with a copy of the plans and first confirm that all items have been installed per the drawings. Then you need to review all the installation craftsmanship. This takes time. I'm not able to properly construct a punch list with a contractor breathing down my neck. You likely won't be able to either.

Consider walking the space and creating your punch list on your own time. Once the punch list is complete, walk your store with the contractor, showing him exactly what items your punch list is referencing. Be clear on expectations for satisfactory completion of work, because an owner's and a contractor's expectations of what constitutes a job done right are not always aligned.

It's okay if your punch list gets long. You've paid good money for a project to be done right. All the small stuff truly adds up. Workers should be held accountable for performing adequate work. We all know what acceptable craftsmanship looks like, yet there's not always enforcement of standard, resulting in corners being cut (figuratively and literally) and subpar work performed.

Don't just do a visual punch walk. Use your hands, ears, nose, and senses. Run faucets for 30 seconds, and then look under the sink for drips. Feel the sturdiness of counters. Test doors to make sure they latch properly and don't slam shut. Listen for rattling systems. Use your nose to detect leaking fluids or sewer gas.

### Lien Waivers

Once construction is complete, punch list items have been redressed, and you've paid the contractor in full, it's time to request unconditional lien waivers from the GC. What's an unconditional lien waiver? According to Scott Wolfe Jr. of Levelset.com, "An [unconditional] lien waiver is a document from a contractor, subcontractor, material supplier, equipment rental company, or other parties (a potential lien claimant) to the construction project stating that they waive future lien rights against the property improved to the extent (the amount of money) set forth in the waiver. You can think of lien waivers as the construction industry's version of a receipt for payment" [18].

You'll need lien waivers from all subcontractors, supplies, and the general contractor. Your GC should spearhead this process. A lien waiver is more than just proof of payment; it acknowledges that the entity signing it will not come after you for outstanding balances tied to the construction of your business.

If you do not receive lien waivers, an entity could file a mechanical lien against the property. A mechanical lien is a claim that an entity involved in the construction of your store was not paid for their services.

Even though you may have paid the general contractor in full, a subcontractor or supplier may place a mechanical lien on your property. Why? Because suppliers and subcontractors don't contract with you, they contract with the general contractor, and sometimes general contractors fail to pay their subcontractors. If a court determines the entity was not paid in full, you or the landlord will be liable for paying the subcontractor the remainder of their outstanding balance, even if you've already paid the GC in whole. It's not fair, but that's the way of the road.

Since unpaid entities often place mechanical liens on the actual building a tenant leases from a landlord, a landlord may become legally culpable for paying the mechanical lien. Because of this, most landlords will not disburse tenant improvement allowances until they have copies of all lien waivers—another reason to get those lien waivers ASAP!

**Operating Systems and Manuals**

Following routine maintenance is an important part of store operations. Just as a car should be serviced at routine intervals, so should your store's systems. A contractor should provide all applicable maintenance procedures and schedules for systems they installed upon the completion of construction. Have the contractor provide a rundown of what systems require maintenance, tune-ups, or inspections, and at what frequency. Next, set up recurring e-calendar reminders for said maintenance. Deferring maintenance leads to unpleasant costs and headaches down the road.

Below are examples of general system maintenance for restaurants. After the first scheduled maintenance of each system, review the necessary frequency for follow-up maintenance.

1. **HVAC:** quarterly system check and air filter replacement
2. **HVAC economizers:** semiannual review to confirm working conditions
3. **Hood:** daily wipe-down, daily baffle cleaning, quarterly filter swap, quarterly grease duct and grease exhaust fan cleaning
4. **Grease trap:** quarterly system pump
5. **Refrigeration:** quarterly condenser coil cleaning, quarterly air filter check, quarterly drainage pipe

and drainage pan cleaning, annual refrigerant-level check

6. **Water filter(s):** quarterly replacement
7. **Dishwasher:** daily filter clean, annual inspection and recalibration

**Development Checklist**

We've run through a multitude of tasks and activities that must be completed at specific times during a store's development to avoid cost overruns and project delays. In addition to the items listed in this book there are self-evident items (such as setting up phone and internet service) that are important to be cognizant of to avoid project delays. On my website—blairramsing.com—you'll find an editable version of a generic development checklist that you can tweak to suite your concept's needs.

Given the many tasks involved in opening a retail store, odds are good that without a development checklist, tasks will be forgotten and information misplaced. A checklist is a great organizational tool. If you've brought on a business partner or consultant, give them access to your checklist and upload it to a website that shows real-time edits (such as Google Docs) so that everyone is working off the latest and greatest information.

Good luck in your endeavors!

# IN CLOSING

If you've found value in these pages, please consider spreading the word about this book so that others can also learn the do's, don'ts, and general steps of building a business.

To echo the opening words:


After reading the book, feel free to leave a note on my website with questions or comments. Nobody's perfect. I'm far from it. If you believe I've made an error or omission, I'd love to hear from you:
www.blairramsing.com

My website also provides a breakdown of service offerings for anyone in need of assistance or consultation during the development of their store.

# TIPS, TRICKS, INSIGHTFUL QUOTES, AND MISCELLANEOUS JUNK

Having trouble getting ahold of someone? Send them an e-calendar meeting invitation with a call-in conference number. The key is to make the meeting invitation send a reminder to the recipient 10 minutes before the call. I've had a surprisingly high success rate at getting ahold of busy clients, city officials, design professionals, and contractors by doing this. I believe the success is in part because many people connect their work calendar to their phone, with meeting invitations and reminders showing up on their phone as push notifications.

*Life is 10% what happens to you and 90% how you react to it.*—Charles R. Swindoll

Are you about to pay dark rent, or did you run into an unexpected financial snag? A smart landlord knows they're successful only if you're successful. Since landlords have a vested interest in your success, they're more receptive than you'd think to extending free-rent periods or helping pay an unexpected $10,000 water tap fee, *even when they don't have to.* It never hurts to ask. The worst that can happen is they say no.

*Your most unhappy customers are your greatest source of learning.*—Bill Gates

The president of one of the five largest pizza chains once told me that the biggest difference between successful store owners and their counterparts is best reflected in how the owners allocate their time and invest in their employees. The operator who spends most of her time growing the business from outside the store's four walls and invests extra capital to retain high-quality staff is the owner who's markedly more successful than the operator who focuses inward and fails to invest in adequate personnel.

*Your attitude, not your aptitude, will determine your altitude.*—Zig Ziglar

Are there people who scrape by in the beginning and make it? Sure, but those folks are few and far between. Undercapitalized businesses tend to spiral downward. Financial prudence and fiscal responsibility are paramount to the success of any business, *but* having sufficient start-up capital is equally important. Make sure you have contingency funds to tap into in the event that you find yourself among the majority of new businesses that spend more money than originally budgeted.

If you've never done something before, John Maynard Keynes says, "It is better to be roughly right than precisely wrong."

Know what you should and should not spend your time perfecting.
*In business, perfection is the enemy of profitability.*—Marc Cuban

# Works Cited

[1] The Office of Advocacy. "Frequently Asked Questions About Small Business," August 2018. [https://www.sba.gov/sites/default/files/advocacy/Frequently-Asked-Questions-Small-Business-2018.pdf]. Accessed 29 April 2019.

[2] SSRS. goldmansachs.com, June 2016. [https://www.goldmansachs.com/citizenship/10000-small-businesses/US/news-and-events/babson-small-businesses/multimedia/babson-state-of-small-business-in-america-report.pdf]. Accessed 29 April 2019.

[3] B. T. Yates. Analyzing Costs, Procedures, Processes, and Outcomes in Human Services, vol. 42, SAGE, 1996.

[4] D. Galorath. "Why Can't People Estimate: Estimation Bias and Mitigation," 2015. conference.usu.edu. Accessed 29 April 2019.

[5] RS Means. January 2019. [https://www.rsmeansonline.com/references/unit/refpdf/hci.pdf]. rsmeansonline.com. Accessed 29 April 2019.

[6] C. N. M. G. LLC. usinflationcalculator.com, 2008–2018. [https://www.usinflationcalculator.com/inflation/current-inflation-rates/]. Accessed 29 April 2019.

[7] Mortenson. "4th Quarter 2018 Mortenson Construction Cost Index—Seattle, WA," 2019. [https://www.mortenson.com/~/media/files/pdfs/cost%20index%20report%20-%20seattle%20-%20q4%202018.ashx]. Accessed 29 April 2019.

[8] Gordian. *2019 Building Construction Costs with RSMeans*

*Data*, 7. a. edition, Ed., 2019. Book

[9] Mortenson. "4th Quarter 2018 Mortenson Construction Cost Index—Denver, CO," 2019. [https://www.mortenson.com/~/media/files/pdfs/cost%20index%20report%20-%20denver%20-%20q4%202018.ashx]. Accessed 29 April 2019.

[10] Merriam-Webster. [Online]. Accessed 29 April 2019.

[11] U.S. Small Business Administration. "Loan Fact Sheet," October 2011. [https://www.sba.gov/sites/default/files/SDOLoanFactSheet_Oct_2011.pdf]. Accessed 29 April 2019.

[12] Access. "The Impact of Retail Proximity on Consumer Purchases," 2017. [https://cdn2.hubspot.net/hubfs/263750/Access_Consumer_Spend_Study_2016.pdf]. Accessed 29 April 2019.

[13] Based on a review of 30 different tenant improvement projects I analyzed, 2018.

[14] K. Graddy. "What's Your Sign?" FedEx, 2012. [https://about.van.fedex.com/blog/whats-your-sign-not-just-a-conversation-opener/]. Accessed 29 April

[15] Larimer County Colorado Building Department. "Temporary Certificates of Occupancy (TCO)," 1 August 14. [Online]. Accessed 29 April 2019.

[16] Bright Local. "Local Consumer Review Survey," 7 December 2018. [https://www.brightlocal.com/learn/local-consumer-review-survey/?SSAID=314743&SSCID=21k3_jry89]. Accessed 29 April 2019.

[17] Korn Ferry. "Retail Employee Turnover Up as Black Friday and Holiday Shopping Season Nears, According to Korn Ferry Survey of Top U.S. Retailers," 15 November 2012. [https://ir.kornferry.com/node/15596/pdf]. Accessed 29 April 2019.

[18] Scott Wolfe, Jr ."The Ultimate Guide to Lien Waivers." 29 March 2019. [https://blog.zlien.com/construction-payment/ultimate-guide-to-lien-waivers/]. Accessed 29 April 2019.

Made in the USA
Monee, IL
27 June 2021